ALAMEDA
California Crossroads

Pictorial research by David Lewis Wright
"Partners in Progress" by Frederick J. Monteagle
Produced in cooperation with the Alameda County Historical Society
Windsor Publications, Inc.
Northridge, California

ALAMEDA
California Crossroads

AN ILLUSTRATED HISTORY

Ruth Hendricks Willard

This book is lovingly dedicated to
Alameda County children of all ages,
heirs to a rich and cosmopolitan legacy,

and especially to

Adam and Anne
Patricia and Gayle
Richard and Paul
and Will

"These became part of that child
who went forth every day
and who now goes,
and will always go forth every day."
—Walt Whitman

Windsor Publications, Inc.—History Books Division

Managing Editor: Karen Story
Design Director: Alexander D'Anca

Staff for *Alameda County*

Manuscript Editor: Marilyn Horn
Photo Editor: Lynne Ferguson Chapman
Production Editors: Amy Adelstein, Robin Mastrogeorge
Historical Consultants: Denzil Verardo and Jennie Dennis Verardo
Editor, Corporate Biographies: Brenda Berryhill
Production Editor, Corporate Biographies: Una FitzSimons
Senior Proofreader: Susan J. Muhler
Editorial Assistants: Didier Beauvoir, Thelma Fleischer, Kim Kievman, Rebecca Kropp, Michael Nugwynne, Kathy B. Peyser, Pat Pittman, Theresa Solis
Sales Representatives, Corporate Biographies: Dave Cook, Liz Cook
Layout Artists: Dan Irwin, Christina Rosepapa
Layout Artist, Corporate Biographies: Mari Catherine Preimesberger
Designer: Tanya Maiboroda

Library of Congress Cataloging-in-Publication Data

Willard, Ruth Hendricks.
    Alameda County, California crossroads: an illustrated history/by Ruth Hendricks Willard; pictorial research by David Lewis Wright; "Partners in progress" by Frederick J. Monteagle.
    "Produced in cooperation with the Alameda County Historical Society."
    Bibliography: p. 129
    Includes index.
    ISBN: 0-89781-283-2
    1. Alameda County (Calif.)—History. 2. Alameda County (Calif.)—Description travel—Views. 3. Alameda County (Calif.)—Industries. I. Wright, David Lewis. II. Alameda County Historical Society. III. Title.
F868.A3W54 1988
979.4'65—dc19   88-21619
                                  CIP

©1988 Windsor Publications, Inc.
All rights reserved
Published 1988
Printed in the United States of America
First Edition

Windsor Publications, Inc.
Elliot Martin, Chairman of the Board
James L. Fish, III, Chief Operating Officer
Hal Silverman, Vice-President/Publisher

CONTENTS

PREFACE

If, as wrote the astronaut Michael Collins, "Earth is God's grand experiment," California may well be foremost among the laboratories in which human culture is forged. And, to a remarkable degree, the events and circumstances of that state's tumultuous history are part and parcel of the Alameda County story.

Attempting to capture within two covers the essence of so diverse and dynamic an area might be likened to trying to hold a moonbeam in one's hand. Volumes much longer than this have been published on most of the individual communities. Rather than a definitive history, then, this work is an attempt to highlight the forces, events, and personalities of the county's exciting past, challenging present, and probable future.

Like all such books, this one derives its character from the many persons who have given generously of their time to provide information and assist with interpretation. Those who have provided special help include, first of all, Senator Arthur H. Breed, Jr., Frances Buxton, Peter Conmy, Douglas Kyle, and Bernadine Swadley of the Alameda County Historical Society, without whose gracious assistance and sponsorship this book could not have been published.

For overall knowledge and assistance throughout the entire project, none can compare with William Sturm, librarian of the Oakland Public Library's outstanding Oakland History Room. For valued advice and editorial suggestions, I thank historical consultants Jennie Dennis Verardo, a social historian, and Denzil Verardo, an expert on political movements.

Sincere appreciation is due to the following people for sharing their specialized knowledge: Jerome H. Pressler, Ohlone College; Donald Savage, University of California; Chuck Cecil, California Academy of Sciences; Rupert Costo, American Indian Historical Association; Philip Galvan, honorary chief of the Ohlone tribe; Dolores Ferenz, Mission San Jose; John S. Sandoval, authority on southern Alameda County; Cecilia Weed, Alameda County Parks, Recreation, and Historical Commission; Tom Kitayama, mayor of Union City; Patrick Skelton and Karen Sweet, Alameda County Fair Association; Mel Wax, Port of Oakland; David Giri, Hindu Temple; Gayle Reynolds, Berkeley Architectural Heritage Association; Joseph Armstrong Baird, Jr., architectural historian; and Frances Keller and Stanley Andersen, San Francisco State University. The theme quotation was located by the Bay Area Reference Center, San Francisco Public Library, and supplied by the NASA History Office, National Aeronautics and Space Administration. The many fine institutions supplying information are listed in a special Appendix.

Working with colleagues David Wright and Monte Monteagle has been a joyful experience. I thank Marilyn Horn, manuscript editor, and Lynne Ferguson Chapman, photo editor, of Windsor Publications for their skillful guidance during the long period of preparation. And last but far from least, I thank Will Willard, who generously devoted his first year of retirement to acting as my capable research assistant.

Small lakes and ponds dot the arroyo of Shadow Cliffs Regional Recreation Area. Only a mile from downtown Pleasanton, Shadow Cliffs was donated to the East Bay Regional Park District by Kaiser Industries. Courtesy, East Bay Regional Park District

Founded on June 11, 1797, Mission San Jose is the oldest European settlement in the East Bay. This 1936 photograph shows the wooden Gothic church built after the earthquake of 1868 and since replaced by a replica of the 1809 adobe church. Courtesy, Pacific Aerial Surveys

INTRODUCTION

From the beginnings of recorded time, and even long before, men, women, and children, earthbound, have observed the brilliance and the movements of the heavenly bodies and wondered about their nature and significance. A little after the middle of the 20th century, finally able to overcome the limitations of gravity, a few representatives of the human race ventured into space. For the first time, Earth itself could be viewed from afar.

To one of these, Michael Collins, fell the responsibility of manning the command module while his fellow astronauts Neil A. Armstrong and Edwin Aldrin took that "giant leap for mankind" by setting foot on the moon for the first time. Collins described the awesome experience with eloquence:

Yet as our vehicles probe space, we know that our small planet is in fact one of a kind. All other environments in the solar system are unimaginably forbidding and hostile. It is as if Earth were God's grand experiment, a unique garden which He has given us to use and enjoy . . . Suddenly I was aware of a shift in my attitude toward Earth. I remembered what it was like down there when I walked her surface— such a splendor of diversity, such richness of color and of life.

It would be difficult indeed to find a portion of Earth's garden more splendidly diverse, more richly, colorfully endowed, than the 733 square miles of land and 92.4 square miles of water roughly centered at 37 degrees 39 minutes north latitude, 122 degrees 5 minutes west longitude, and bordering virtually the entire continental shoreline of San Francisco Bay. Passageways through the rugged hills on the east link the coastal region with the riches of the continent beyond. Whether considering scenic beauty, the tangible evidence of human activity, or the invisible but ever-present electricity of human thought, Alameda County, California, leads the way in sheer variety.

With that explosive combination of events in 1848—the discovery of gold and the American annexation of California—the great bay and the mountain passes provided a convergence of natural thoroughfares through which poured one of the greatest voluntary migrations in the history of humankind. And ever since that time the spectacular setting, fertile land, and friendly climate have continued to attract as diverse and talented a population as ever learned to coexist anywhere. The products of their fields and factories are important in world commerce; the philosophical and scientific advances pioneered by the University of California have altered American and world culture irrevocably. Here, at the edge of the continent, the land meets the sea, the great march of Western civilization comes full circle to confront its Eastern counterpart, and two great tectonic plates of the Earth's crust continue their ancient and relentless combat.

What manner of land, what manner of people have contributed to this "world oasis, flawed paradise, lifestyle crucible, and creative milieu"? What giant forces flooded, elevated, eroded, folded, and tossed the Earth so repeatedly and so violently that seashells, whale bones, and beach boulders can be found on hilltops far above the present level of the sea, while the fossilized bones of ancient land mammals are turned up 80 feet below the estuary floor and deep in the bowels of the Berkeley Hills during excavations for 20th-century tunnels?

What adverse winds, offshore currents, and impenetrable fog banks hid the magnificent harbor from seafaring explorers for more than 150 years, and then revealed its secrets at a time when the resources of the Spanish Crown were so depleted that its minions were unable to explore and develop more than a shallow segment of the coastline? What quirks of fate concealed the gold from that rigidly authoritarian power and then revealed it to the vanguard of the first society on the face of the globe to espouse the doctrines of religious freedom and open immigration?

Clues to the riddles—with the exception of the last—are everywhere. They are evident within the vortex of human activity that is Alameda County today; in the melodious place names, romantic adobes, and colorful social customs that recall the Hispanic period; and also in the few surviving village sites, bedrock mortars, shell mounds, and salt marshes used by the original human inhabitants, the Ohlone Indians. They can also be found in the Earth itself.

With 5,924 acres of grassland and oak woods, and a diversity of plants and animals, the Sunol Regional Wilderness is a center of study of Alameda County's rich natural history. Courtesy, East Bay Regional Park District

A Unique Garden to Use and Enjoy

The word *alameda* means "a grove or lane of poplar trees." The county undoubtedly took the name from its largest creek, *El Arroyo de la Alameda* (Alameda Creek), so christened by its European discoverers because its course, lined with willows and sycamores, resembled the *alamedas* or tree-lined roadways of Spain.

There were numerous other creeks in the early days, tumbling down the hillsides to the bay. Some of the original streams have been dammed for irrigation or recreation; others have disappeared underground. And the hill-sides are now mainly occupied by residential neighborhoods.

Today's landscape reflects primarily the aspirations and activities—the footprints as it were—of the area's residents since it became a part of the American West. But it also reveals the imprints of two earlier cultures. Place names, architecture, plantings, boundary lines, and highway routes afford ample evidence of an earlier Hispanic culture as well as glimpses into the lives of the indigenous people whose world began to crumble with the arrival of the first Europeans in 1769.

This portion of Earth's garden is highly unusual if not unique in the amount of mobility that went into its formation, and the visible evidence of past living inhabitants. So plentiful, in fact, are the fossilized fragments of pre-human existence that it is hard to pick up a rock in Alameda County without holding a bit of prehistoric life in one's hand.

TERRA NON FIRMA

The county is bordered by mountains on the east and salt water on the west. This meeting of land and sea is included within the zone of earthquake and volcanic activity known as the Pacific Rim of Fire. In California the usually mild but sometimes violent tremors are caused by lateral movements along a group of active earthquake faults. Much of Alameda County, the bay, and most of San Francisco rest upon a separate shard of the Earth's crust, sand-wiched between the San Andreas and Hayward faults.

While earthquake faults are the most fa-mous geological feature of California, they are far from the oldest. Perhaps five billion years ago, the newly formed planet was a swirling, sizzling mass of molten rock and gasses. As the surface cooled, the magma hardened into crustal plates, floating on the still-liquid inte-rior, and seas were formed of liquid methane, ammonia, and water. After nearly three-quarters of the Earth's history had passed, the first organic molecules appeared.

As the huge plates moved about, land-masses were upthrust, only to begin the process of leveling as weathering, sedimentation, and erosion carried fragments back to the sea. More than 65 million years ago the Pacific Plate, moving in an easterly direction, began sliding beneath the North American Plate, pushing up the early Sierra Nevada and Coast

Ranges. These collisions continued intermittently for some 40 million years.

Subduction ended 25-10 million years ago, as the Pacific Plate began moving in a northwesterly direction. In the past 70,000 years the oceanic plate has crept northward about 2,000 miles from its earlier position off the west coast of Mexico.

The extra thrust along the continental edge intensified the folding and buckling of the Oakland-Berkeley Hills, lifted up San Francisco peninsula above the sea, and flooded the Central Valley. As the two sides of a fault grind against one another, the friction builds until finally it is released in an earthquake. Alameda County's most important fault, the Hayward, runs from Pt. Pinole Regional Shoreline in Richmond to Mt. Misery near San Jose.

The extensive flooding deposited several thousand feet of sediment, most of it fossiliferous, in the Mt. Diablo area. Evidence of large-scale folding and contortion of the oceanic sediments can be seen on road and quarry cuts. The most ancient fossils, minute marine organisms called radiolaria, date back more than 100 million years. Here, in this temperate climate, are shells of extinct snails, clams, oysters, and ammonites from tropical seas, and subtropical species of oysters, corals, and scallops. The county's oldest record of plant life—leaf prints of subtropical ferns, palms, magnolias, and avocados—are found in the coal beds at Tesla.

With the onset of the Pliocene period (11.7 million years ago) the marine waters began their final retreat, and land mammals appeared. Excavations carried on at the University of California's Blackhawk Fossil Preserve give an almost complete picture of life during the Pliocene. Herds of mastodons, camels, antelopes, and small three-toed horses grazed on the grassy plain. Other inhabitants included peccaries, primitive wolverines, big cats resembling mountain lions, rabbits, squirrels, beavers, cranes, and lizards. A primitive rhinoceros was uncovered by workmen excavating for the Caldecott Tunnel.

From 10 to seven million years ago volcanoes reshaped the terrain with explosive force, spewing molten lava, ash, cinders, and rock fragments over the landscape. Basaltic lava can be seen along Grizzly Peak Boulevard and east of the Caldecott Tunnel. Extinct volcanic craters have been preserved at Sibley Regional Volcanic Preserve. Meanwhile the San Francisco Bay plate continued to list downward. The San Joaquin and Sacramento rivers merged and chiseled their way to the sea through the present Golden Gate.

During the Pleistocene epoch (three million to 10,000 years ago) monstrous glaciers intermittently locked much of the northern hemisphere in ice and snow. As the glaciers expanded, the sea level fell, exposing a land (or ice) bridge across the Bering Strait. Herds of large mammals drifted across the isthmus from Asia, moving slowly southward to California, where they mingled with others that had crossed the Panama corridor from South America. Bones of the Columbian mammoth were found during construction of the Posey Tube. The most extensive collection of early Pleistocene fauna in North America occurs in the Irvington gravel pits. These fossils predate those of the La Brea Tar Pits by more than 600,000 years.

The stage was being readied for the momentous year of 1848. Glaciers, volcanoes, and earthquakes continued to remodel the mountain ranges. Underground watercourses, their routes blocked by seismic activity, burst to the surface bearing particles of a shiny mineral and began carving new pathways to the sea. Fed by melting glacial ice, the sea level rose 300 feet and the Pacific Ocean poured through the Golden Gate, creating San Francisco Bay. Incentive and opportunity awaited the arrival of modern man.

FOOTSTEPS IN THE GARDEN

The earliest craft to ply the waters of San Francisco Bay were tule balsa canoes, made by descendants of the intrepid men and women who crossed the Aleutian land bridge and spread out across North America, developing regional cultures and languages as time went by. Human habitation in the Alameda County area began some 6,000 years ago. These earliest residents spoke local dialects of the Penutian language.

The Spanish called them *Costeños* (coast people), which was quickly corrupted to Cos-

tanoans. Their preferred name for themselves is Ohlone, referring to either a community south of Oakland or a Miwok word meaning "the western people."

Early European accounts describe them as rather short of stature, with dark skin, brown eyes, and straight black hair. The women wore short skirts or aprons of deerskin or vegetable fibers, tatooed their faces, and frequently put flowers in their hair. The men were lightly bearded and usually naked, although in cold weather they sometimes smeared mud over their bodies. They sometimes painted their faces and bodies with earth colors, and wore ceremonial headdresses fashioned of beach pebbles, feathers, bones, leather, and shells.

The chief was a leader revered for his wisdom but without the power of life and death over his tribesmen. Shamans within each group treated injuries and disease with great skill. All their activities were governed by a reverence for nature inherited from their Creator Gods, who made the Earth and then left it in the care of the human beings.

They were basically sedentary people, occupying the same village site for generations. Dwellings and granaries were round, reed-thatched structures. As hunters and harvesters, they found ample foodstuffs in the forests, the creeks, the salt marshes, and the bay, with the plentiful acorn providing the staple of their diet. From such natural materials as stone, bone, shell, leather, and sinew, they fashioned a wide variety of tools. Watertight baskets woven of roots and grasses served as containers and, by dropping heated stones into baskets of water, as cooking utensils.

Each village had its *temescal*, or sweat house, a thatched hut covered with mud and similar to a sauna in function. Each day the men of the village built a fire inside and after working up a sweat, plunged into a nearby stream. The Spanish name for the area that became Oakland was *Encinal de Temescal*—the oak grove near the sweat house.

The Ohlones left more than 400 shell mounds on the bay and estuary shores. Several have been preserved in Coyote Hills Regional Park. These time capsules, containing human burials as well as the debris of daily living, reveal a people who lived in peace with their neighbors, never developing any weapons beyond the tools necessary for daily life.

Although the Ohlones lived in harmony

Alameda County's Ohlone Indians crossed San Francisco Bay in reed boats. The Ohlones tied three bundles of tules together to make the craft. This image was drawn circa 1816 by Louis Choris, a member of the Otto Kotzebue expedition to California. Courtesy, Bancroft Library, University of California, Berkeley

XII

Above: The Ohlone Indians were the first inhabitants of what would become Alameda County. Nature provided all the materials the Ohlones needed to produce the necessities of life, as well as ornamental headdresses and body paints. Courtesy, California Historical Society

Right: This tule house under construction at the Sunol Regional Wilderness Area shows the willow framework and covering of tule mats as used by the Ohlone Indians. The popularity of this pilot project led naturalists to build an Ohlone village in the park. Two or three times during the year, the public is invited to assist with rebuilding the dwellings, granaries, and sweathouse of the village. Photo by Lee Foster

Mission San Jose, founded in 1797, is the cradle of Christianity in Alameda County. This replica of the 1809 adobe chapel, built by volunteers and dedicated in 1985, serves the members of St. Joseph's Parish for baptisms, weddings, funerals, and weekday services. Photo by Mark E. Gibson

with nature, they did modify the environment. Observing that certain areas became more fruitful after fires, they periodically conducted controlled burnings that kept the forest floors free of tinder, giving the woodlands a park-like appearance that amazed the Europeans.

FOR CROSS AND FOR CROWN

The recorded history of Alameda County begins with the Sacred Expedition of 1769 led by Gaspar de Portolá. On November 2, 1769, while hunting for fresh game, Sergeant Francisco Ortega caught sight of the southern reaches of San Francisco Bay and the shoreline now included in Washington Township. To this whole shore Portolá gave the name *Contra Costa,* the "opposite coast." Father Juan Crespi, the expedition diarist, took out his log book and penned these prescient words:

We all held the opinion, without any doubts, that this is a very great and magnificent port. This large, this most noble harbor, is surrounded by high mountains throughout its entire extent, so that it becomes a lake, as it were, protected from all winds. In a word, it is a vast and magnificent harbor, such that not only all the navy of our Most Catholic Majesty, but those of all Europe could take shelter in it.

The Spanish, not content to settle by this harbor, continued to search for a land route to the great bay described in the journals of Sir Francis Drake. Portolá dispatched Ortega, eight soldiers, and an escort of Indians in search of a passage to Point Reyes by way of the Contra Costa. Ortega was given four days to traverse the area. He found no inland route.

And so it was that Spanish leather left its mark on the soil of Alameda County. Within the next seven years, five more expeditions reconnoitered present-day Alameda and Contra Costa counties. But it would take many years before the first and only mission was established on the Contra Costa.

In 1795 Sergeant Pedro Amador recommended a mission site at the place he called "Alameda." This is the earliest officially documented reference to that designation. The Ohlones called the place Oroysom, and it lay on

a natural highway to the valley of the San Joaquin River. The abundant natural resources included well-watered, fertile ground, stones and redwoods in the nearby foothills, and adobe soil suitable for building.

Mission San Jose, 14th of the Alta California missions, was founded on June 11, 1797, by Father Fermin Francisco de Lasuen. Within days Fathers Isidoro Barcenilla and Agustín Merino arrived to take charge. It was their responsibility to bring to the inhabitants of the Contra Costa both Christian salvation and Spanish culture, and they went about their work with great earnestness. A corporal and six soldiers were assigned to maintain order, protect the priests, and punish any Indians who raided cattle herds or cornfields.

There were 33 converts by the end of 1797, and by 1800 the mission had a population of 286 neophytes, "large stock" numbering 367, 1,600 sheep and goats, and 1,500 bushels of crops, chiefly wheat.

The golden years of Mission San Jose began in 1806 with the arrival of Fathers Narcisco Durán and Buenaventura Fortuni. They accelerated the building program already begun, completing the church in 1809. A two-story rectory containing schoolrooms, workshops, storehouses, and sleeping cells was followed by adobe houses for neophyte families, a dormitory for unmarried Indian maidens, a barracks, and a guardhouse.

In 1814 the padres dammed Mission Creek, building a water-powered gristmill as well as a reservoir for the extensive gardens, orchards, vineyards, and olive groves. A large granary stored reserves of wheat, barley, and corn. They expanded the herds of cattle and sheep, locating herders' camps at what are now Hayward, San Leandro, Alameda, and San Antonio Embarcadero in East Oakland.

By 1826 the resident Indian population had grown to 1,886, and the mission was operating a tannery, a soap factory, and a weaving operation that turned out 150 blankets and nine serapes a week. An accomplished musician, Durán trained a 30-piece all-Indian orchestra whose performances on homemade drums, flutes, violins, and trumpets were in great demand at community affairs.

Daily life at the mission included religious instruction, work, and relaxation. Women were taught dressmaking, knitting, weaving, embroidering, laundering, and cooking. The men learned to plow, sow, cultivate, reap, thresh, and glean, as well as how to build adobe houses, tan leather hides, shear sheep, weave rugs and clothing from the wool, and make ropes, soap, paint, and other useful articles.

The number of baptisms at Mission San Jose exceeded that of any other mission. Epidemics of European diseases, however, caused the Indian death rates to soar, despite efforts by the missionaries and some settlers to provide health care.

Sometimes neophytes ran away or failed to return from visits to their native rancherias, or villages. In 1828 a Mission San Jose *alcalde* (chief) with the baptismal name Estanislao (Stanislaus) led a group of runaways whom the padres suspected of planning a general uprising against the mission program. Soldiers under Mariano Vallejo put the armed Indians to flight after killing a great many of them, both warriors and women. Stanislaus fled to the mission, where Durán gave him sanctuary. The river and the county where the major engagements took place are named for him.

In 1834, after Mexico became independent from Spain, the missions were secularized. The missions were turned into parish churches and the clergy's authority limited to religious matters. In theory half the property was to be given to the former neophytes and half handled by lay administrators. In actuality, since very few Indians were able to cope with independent land ownership and the land was coveted by others, most of the mission lands soon passed into private hands.

Soon after the secularization a small rancheria was set aside for the Indians near present-day Fairmont Hospital. In 1840 the village was officially recognized by the governor, and the land was specifically excluded from the surrounding ranchos. The little "tribe" planted corn and beans, and managed to survive "until wiped out by eating squirrels poisoned by the settlers." Old Umbry, the sole survivor, died near San Leandro in 1873. As late as 1904 other Indians occupied small rancherias at secluded spots along the Alameda canyon and near Pleasanton.

The earthquake of 1868 destroyed virtually the entire mission quadrangle. A frame

Father Narcisco Durán was one of the most prominent friars of Alta California, as widely respected for his administrative skills as for his missionary work. He served at Mission San Jose from 1809-1834 and then at Mission Santa Barbara until his death in 1846. The published account of Eugene Duflot de Mofrá's visit to California in 1841-1842 contained this lithograph of Father Durán and an Ohlone child. Courtesy, Bancroft Library, University of California, Berkeley

Gothic church and rectory erected on the site served until 1973, when volunteers began plans to duplicate the original church. The rectory was relocated to nearby Anza Street and the church sold to an Anglican congregation who restored it for use in San Mateo.

After extensive research and planning a replica of the 1809 adobe church arose on the original stone foundation. The richly decorated interior follows descriptions in the inventories of the 1830s. The four original bells hang in the belfry. Of the several interments under the red tile floor of the church, the only marker found was that of Robert Livermore. Other pioneers lie buried in the adjacent cemetery. A surviving portion of the old adobe rectory (the oldest building in Alameda County) serves as a museum and visitors' center.

About a mile west on Washington Boulevard is the Ohlone burial ground. On January 6, 1965, Bishop Floyd L. Begin of the diocese of Oakland presented the old cemetery to the American Indian Historical Society for restoration. Although there are no full-blooded Ohlones, about 250 descendants of mixed blood live in the area. Among the most faithful caretakers is Philip Galvan, who is often referred to as the chief of the Ohlones.

THE RANCHO PERIOD

Under Spanish rule, large landholdings called ranchos were bestowed as a reward for loyal service or to stimulate settlement of new areas.

Each recipient was obligated to build a permanent dwelling and either farm or raise stock on the land, whose title remained with the Crown.

The only Spanish land grant entirely within Alameda County was Rancho San Antonio, bestowed in August 1820 upon Luis Maria Peralta, who came to California with the Anza Expedition of 1776 and served in the army for 40 years. At the time of the grant he was *comisionado* of the pueblo of San Jose, where he continued to live. Nearly 45,000 acres in size, the rancho included 13 miles of shoreline from San Leandro Creek to El Cerrito Creek and stretched east to the summits of the Oakland-Berkeley Hills.

In August 1842 Peralta divided the rancho among his four sons as follows: to Domingo, the northernmost portion (Albany and Berkeley); to Vicénte, the Encinal de Temescal (Emeryville, North and Central Oakland, and Piedmont); to Antonio, the site of the original adobe in East Oakland as well as all of Alameda; to Ignacio, the southernmost portion including parts of Oakland and San Leandro.

Outright grants of land began in the Mexican era. A Mexican citizen could petition for up to a square league of irrigated land, four leagues dependent upon rainfall only, and six leagues for grazing cattle by defining the area with a verbal description and a *diseño* (sketch map) and showing cause why he should receive it. Foreigners who had assumed Mexican citizenship and adopted the Catholic faith were also eligible.

Briefly, the Mexican ranchos of Alameda County were these:

Rancho San Ramon was granted in August 1835 to José Maria Amador, a retired soldier who had served as majordomo at Mission San Jose in 1827. The 16,516 acres of prime land extended from Dublin into Contra Costa County. Amador trained his Indian and Mexican vaqueros to manufacture wagons, saddles, harnesses, shoes, blankets, soap, and other commodities. After the discovery of gold at Coloma in 1848 he and a company of Indians engaged in a highly successful mining operation in the area later named for him. At one time Amador had 300-400 horses, 13,000-14,000 head of cattle, and 3,000-4,000 sheep.

Rancho Las Positas, consisting of 8,800 acres in the Livermore Valley, was granted in

April 1839 to José Noriega (who later relinquished his interest) and Robert Livermore, an Englishman who had married Josepha Higuera-Molina (the daughter of a Santa Clara County ranchero) but had not yet been granted Mexican citizenship. Livermore planted the first orchards and vineyards outside the mission and built the first frame dwelling in the valley. The rancho became famous for hospitality to visiting travelers and for the whale skeleton and mounds of giant fossilized oyster shells on the property.

Rancho El Valle de San Jose, granted in April 1839, contained 48,436 acres near Pleasanton and was granted to four third-generation Californians: Agustín Bernal, Juan Pablo Bernal, Maria Pilar Bernal (married to Antonio Maria Pico), and Maria Dolores Bernal (wife of Antonio Maria Sunol). The Picos and the Sunols sold their interests to the two Bernals. The Sunols' son lived near today's Sunol Water Temple in the 1840s and early 1850s.

The Bernals were good business managers and responsible citizens. Maria Dolores Bernal Sunol, who devoted much of her time to charity work among the Indians, is the only woman buried under the altar in Mission San Jose. Juan Pablo's daughter Maria Refugia Bernal Kottinger is revered for vaccinating the Indians during a smallpox epidemic.

The 8,800-acre Rancho Santa Rita,

Left: This Rancho San Antonio adobe, built in 1819 at present-day Paxton and Coolidge streets in the Fruitvale district of East Oakland, was the first permanent dwelling (outside the mission) in Alameda County. This adobe was torn down in 1897 and some of the bricks used to build a small house in Dimond Park (East Oakland). Courtesy, Oakland History Room, Oakland Public Library

Below, left: This early nineteeth-century sketch depicts the simple life-style of the rancheros. Note the use of leather straps to hold the corral and cart together. Nails, a scarce commodity, were rarely used for such purposes. Courtesy, Amador-Livermore Valley Historical Society

Cattle ranching was of major importance to Alameda County's settlers during the Mexican period. Vaqueros kept a watchful eye out for strays, lest they be rustled by Indians or bandits. Courtesy, Amador-Livermore Valley Historical Society

granted in April 1839 to José Dolores Pacheco, was choice grazing land on the western edge of the Livermore Valley, adjoining Rancho El Valle de San Jose. Pacheco was prominent in civic affairs in the pueblo of San Jose, where he served as alcalde in 1839.

Rancho San Leandro, granted in 1848, covered 6,830 acres in the Arroyo de San Leandro. The grantee was José de Joaquin Estudillo, a former soldier who had been active in civic affairs, serving in the Provincial Assembly at Monterey (1828-1829) and as a customs official. His family included four foreign sons-in-law. Marie de Jesus married William Heath Davis; Concepcion married John B. Ward; Magdalena married newspaper editor John Nugent; and Dolores married Charles Cushing. By 1852 Estudillo's original herd of 300 heifers had increased tenfold. He specialized in white cattle, whose color, he said, enabled him to see his stock "at a great distance."

There were two divisions of Rancho San Lorenzo, granted in 1841 and 1842. Francisco Soto received the 6,686 acres west of Hayward and south of San Lorenzo Creek. The 26,723 acres in the Hayward-Castro Valley area were

granted to Guillermo Castro, former soldier and also surveyor of lands around Pueblo San Jose. In 1851 his vaqueros reported a gringo pitching a tent on the rancho. Although told to leave, William Hayward convinced the ranchero of his usefulness by making him a pair of boots and was then allowed to buy 40 acres for a dairy.

Rancho de Agua Calientes was granted in 1839 to Fulgencio Higuera. The 9,563 acres were just south of the mission in the area of six warm springs valued by the Indians for their curative powers and utilized (by means of an aqueduct) by the mission population for bathing and laundry. Higuera had served in the army at both San Francisco and San Jose, and in 1837 was a military officer at the pueblo of San Jose.

Rancho Arroyo de la Alameda was granted in 1848 to José de Jesús Vallejo, administrator of Mission San Jose (1836-1840) and brother of Mariano Vallejo. The 17,000 acres lay along Alameda Creek encompassing the Niles and Decoto districts.

Importing stallions from Spain, Vallejo built up a herd of Arabian stock horses that were prized for mounts by the provincial cavalry, the wealthier rancheros, and early American settlers. The tails and manes of the mares were closely cut, and the variously colored hair was skillfully woven and braided by the vaqueros into reins and halters. Early in the 1840s Vallejo built a gristmill that became the nucleus for the settlement of Niles. The vaqueros' adobe on the grant was restored in the 1930s for use as a hospitality house by the California Nursery Company.

Rancho Potrero de Los Cerritos, granted in 1844 to Agustín Alviso and Tomas Pacheco, covered 10,610 acres including much of present-day Union City and all of Newark. Pacheco was a soldier in San Francisco from 1826-1832, and held various posts in the pueblo of San Jose from 1833-1844. Although the grant was made by Governor Manuel Micheltorena, Alviso later participated in the colonists' successful attempt to drive the unpopular governor from office.

The partners at first experienced a year of serious drought, when it was necessary to send the Indians out into the forests to gather branches for the stock to feed on. But after two years of normal rainfall, they were able to export wheat, beans, corn, and cattle to the Russian settlers at Fort Ross and Bodega Bay.

Rancho Ex-Mission San Jose was granted in 1846 by Governor Pio Pico to his brother, Andreas Pico, and the former provisional governor, Juan Bautista Alvarado. The rancho included the last 30,000 acres of Mission San Jose land, encompassing the districts of Mission San Jose, Centerville, and Irvington.

TRANSFORMING THE GARDEN

The rancheros, it seemed, had the best of all possible worlds: fertile soil, a mild climate, ample grazing land, and plenty of vaqueros to perform whatever work could not be done on horseback. While living conditions were unpretentious, social life was spontaneous and carefree. Fall was the highlight of the year, when trading brigs from New England, South America, the Sandwich Islands, and Europe exchanged manufactured goods for the hides and tallow produced by the ranchos.

The Spanish came to a land whose inhabitants had lived for thousands of years in total harmony with nature. Within 70 years, new ways of living had introduced livestock, forage, and other crops needing both irrigation and cultivation. This Garden of Eden, for better or worse, had become one that required tending.

José de Jesús Vallejo built his flour mill in 1841 along the banks of Alameda Creek. The surrounding community was known as Vallejo Mills until 1868. In that year the Central Pacific Railroad developed a plat around the depot and named the town after Judge Addison C. Niles, a major railroad stockholder. Courtesy, Rural Alameda County Collection, California State University, Hayward

An 1853 issue of the Golden Era magazine was one of the earliest publications to extol the virtues of Oakland. Later that year the state legislature created Alameda County from portions of southern Contra Costa and northern Santa Clara counties. Courtesy, California Section, California State Library

THE VILLAGE ERA

Early maps depicted California as an island, and for all practical purposes such was the case through the first half-century of Hispanic occupation. Although the Californians were accustomed to receiving visitors who arrived by sea, it was generally believed impossible to travel overland from the United States to California.

Consequently the arrival in November 1826 at Mission San Gabriel (Los Angeles) of the first Americans—trapper Jedediah Smith and his men—to reach California overland caused great consternation among the Mexican authorities. When some mission Indians defected while Smith's party was camped on the San Joaquin River, Father Durán accused Smith of "enticing my neophytes to desert." Smith defended his presence in a letter to Father Durán but in October 1827 he was detained and taken to Mission San Jose. A release was arranged after Smith agreed to leave and not return south of the 42nd degree latitude.

By contrast the second company of American trappers to visit the mission was warmly welcomed. While camped on the Mokelumne in July 1830, Captain Ewing Young and his men were contacted by Mission San Jose for help in forcibly persuading a group of neophytes to return to the mission. Kit Carson, with the help of 11 trappers and 15 Christian Indians, recaptured the runaways. In appreciation Father Durán arranged the sale of the trappers' entire catch to a Mexican trading brig anchored at Monterey.

By the mid-1840s the trails mapped by these mountain men and the tales they told prompted Americans to follow their dreams to California. A party arriving at Sutter's Fort in 1845 included future Alameda County settlers William Mendenhall and the Smith brothers, Henry C. and Napoleon. After securing Mexican passports at Yerba Buena, these men made lumber and shingles from the redwoods they felled in a nearby grove. When the Peraltas ousted them, they settled in the abandoned buildings at Mission San Jose, where they were soon joined by George Harlan and James Larue.

In July 1846 the schooner *Brooklyn* sailed into San Francisco Bay. The 238 Mormon passengers intended to establish a new Zion under the leadership of Samuel Brannan. The colony failed to materialize, as most of the faithful moved to Utah after the U.S. gained control of California. Several who stayed played major roles in the development of Alameda County. Thomas Eager harvested lumber in the Redwood Canyon area, while John Horner, Earl Marshall, Simeon Stivers, and Origin Mowry sharecropped wheat at Dr. John Marsh's ranch in the Mt. Diablo foothills. While waiting for the wheat to ripen, Horner moved his family into the deserted buildings at the mission.

In 1846 John C. Frémont traversed the East Bay region in connection with a scientific expedition for the U.S. government. As a result of Frémont's presence in California, in June 1846 American settlers captured the town of Sonoma and General Mariano Vallejo, and established the short-lived Bear Flag Republic. Meanwhile the Mexican War was raging, and in July 1846 Commodore John D. Sloat claimed California for the U.S. Troops soon arrived and William Mendenhall and Henry C. Smith enlisted in Frémont's battalion. Sons of the Californio rancheros in this area joined General José Castro's forces in an unsuccessful attempt to stop the American takeover, which was accomplished in early 1848.

When gold was found near Sacramento in 1848, "the world rushed in" to California. Most argonauts came by ship, landing eventually on the Contra Costa. A major route to the mines was established from Mission San Jose through Mission Pass then on to the Sierra foothills via Altamont Pass.

APPORTIONING THE LAND

Although the treaty of Guadalupe Hidalgo, signed at the end of the Mexican War, guaranteed the property rights of Mexican landowners, in Alameda County, perhaps more than any other part of the state, American settlers ignored those rights.

In 1849 the California legislature ruled that any legal settler could appropriate 160 acres of "public land" by fencing, improving, and living on it. But which lands were public? Mexican ranchos tended to be vast holdings with their unfenced boundaries loosely defined. The Americans moved in and assumed control of whatever land looked unoccupied, regardless of prior ownership. José Vallejo filed suit to remove 70 squatters from his land.

The U.S. government set up a land com-

American settlers of the mid-1840s discovered Mission San Jose in a run-down state. Roofs were caved-in and walls were crumbled on many church-owned buildings. Nonetheless some of Alameda County's first settlers housed their families in the abandoned structures. This 1852 painting revealed the progress made in restoration of the site. Courtesy, Mission San Jose Museum

After short excursions to the mines, the early settlers returned to make their fortunes on the east side of San Francisco Bay. Henry C. Smith, alcalde at Mission San Jose, made a great deal of money selling miners' supplies, despite the arrival of a competitor, Elias Lyman Beard, in mid-1849. John Horner found markets for his crops in the mining country and in San Francisco. The area around Mission San Jose, with its active embarcadero and its location on the crossroads, soon had the largest population on the Contra Costa.

mission to confirm preexisting titles, but the burden of proof was upon the original grantees. The settlement of disputes became a long and an expensive process, and most Mexican landowners had to relinquish their property.

Alameda County was formed in 1853 from portions of Santa Clara and Contra Costa counties. The functions of county government were divided between New Haven and Alvarado. Six townships were established and eventually defined as Washington, Eden, Murray, Alameda, Brooklyn, and Oakland.

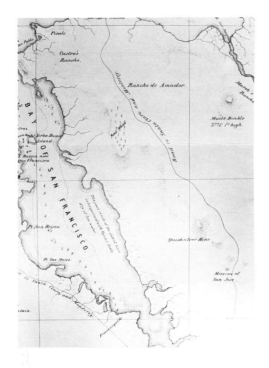

WASHINGTON TOWNSHIP

One of the first American settlers in Washington Township was Elias Lyman Beard. He bought the mission buildings and 28 acres of surrounding orchards from Thomas Larkin, and developed the quadrangle into a showplace where visiting dignitaries were entertained. With John Horner he purchased 30,000 acres of former mission lands on which they planted potatoes. Beard sold his store in 1854 and spent his time extending his orchards, planting vineyards and wheat, operating a gristmill and a wharf on Mission Creek, and serving as the first president of the California State Agricultural Society. When the land commission decreed the reversion of the 28 acres around the quadrangle to the Roman Catholic Church in 1878, Beard and his family moved to a new home on the Niles-Mission San Jose Road.

Above, left: This map of the East Bay dates from 1849. Alameda County was then part of the Contra Costa, the "opposite coast" from San Francisco. From Joseph Warren Revere, Naval Duty in California, 1849. Courtest, Rural Alameda County Collection, California State University, Hayward.

Left: Travelers entering Alameda County from the south found the Warm Springs Hotel and Resort (present-day Fremont) a welcome stop along the way. This scene is from a Lawrence & Houseworth stereoscopic card. Courtesy, California Section, California State Library, Stereo Collection.

Just south of the mission area Clement Columbet developed the Warm Springs Hotel and Resort on land purchased from the Higuera family in 1850. After the buildings were leveled in the earthquake of 1868, Governor Leland Stanford bought the entire area and established an extensive vineyard to supply wine for his railroad and resorts.

Horner continued to expand his holdings, buying land in the Alvarado and Niles areas and building roads between his various farms. His headquarters were at Centerville where he built a store, residence, blacksmith shop, and church/schoolhouse. In 1850 he bought land near the mouth of Alameda Creek from Agustín Alviso, and acquired a small steamship, the *Union,* to make daily deliveries to San Francisco. With the help of his brother William he built piers, warehouses, and a tavern and plotted a townsite. Union City became a distribution center, and the brothers' gross from fruits and vegetables jumped from $150,000 to $270,000. In the fall of 1851 John Horner was named the "First Farmer of California." The Horners eventually sold out and moved to Hawaii to manage a sugar plantation.

In 1851 Henry C. Smith bought 465 acres of land adjoining Union City and started his own town, New Haven. Smith's store in New Haven served as the courthouse until 1854 when the government moved to San Leandro.

Alvarado was established by two San Francisco lawyers, Strode and Jones, in 1852. The adjacent cities of Union City, New Haven, and Alvarado were jointly known as Alvarado for many years. Decoto was part of Alvarado politically from its founding in 1870 to 1898. The Decoto Land Company offered commuter tickets from San Francisco on the Central Pacific Railroad to encourage settlement.

The salt and beet-sugar industries took root in the Alvarado area in the 1860s. John Quigley began processing salt on his 230 acres of shoreline in 1862. In 1865 John Plummer purchased the Turk Island Crystal Salt Works, creating the foundation for Morton Salt's Alameda County operations. The Union Pacific Salt Company, formed in 1868, developed a saltworks at the mouth of Alameda Creek and by the 1880s had become the largest local producer. By the mid-1880s the county's annual production of salt had tripled to 47,000 tons, and by 1900 production reached 100,000 tons.

Ephraim and Ebenezer Dyer first planted sugar beets on their Alvarado farm in 1868, and a year later built a beet-sugar refinery. They incorporated as the Standard Sugar Refining Company and by 1880 employed 125 men producing 100 tons of sugar per day. The Dyer family remained active in the company until 1890, when it became the Alameda Sugar Company.

Irvington, first known as Washington Corners, evolved out of a tavern opened by two black men near the intersection of today's Washington and Fremont boulevards. Nearby Origin Mowry established a highly successful landing on the deep slough just south of Dumbarton Point. Simeon Stivers settled near Lake Elizabeth and shot ducks and geese for San Francisco restaurants. In 1883 Francis Marion "Borax" Smith established a gun club on the lake, but he later moved it to the salt ponds at Coyote Hills. The town was renamed Irvington when the first railroad arrived in 1884.

Niles, at the junction of the San Jose and Stockton branches of the Central Pacific Railroad, was originally known as Vallejo Mills. The community was renamed for a major investor in the railroad, Judge Addison C. Niles.

Niles' nursery business was established when Barclay T. Clough started an almond nursery in 1866. He was soon joined by James

The Bank of Alvarado, Washington Township's first bank, opened for business in 1902 and served the community of almost 600 people. I.V. Ralph was its first president and the institution was capitalized with $25,000. From History of Washington Township, *1904. Courtesy, California Section, California State Library*

Shinn who developed a fruit and ornamental nursery in 1871. The California Nursery moved to Niles in 1881, eventually becoming part of the George Roeding Company, one of the largest nursery companies in the state.

In 1876 Comstock millionaires James G. Fair and James L. Flood joined forces with Alfred D. "Hog" Davis, a farmer and capitalist, to purchase 4,000 acres from the Perrin Brothers Green Point Dairy, including the hamlet of Newark. It was their objective to build a railroad that could compete with the Central Pacific by using the new, lower-cost narrow-gauge equipment. They began by acquiring the Santa Clara Valley Railroad and extending it from Dumbarton Point to Santa Cruz. Soon their ferry, the *Newark,* made daily trips to San Francisco and their South Pacific Coast Railroad offered commuter service to the Alameda Pier. Using advertising and weekend picnics to attract potential residents, the company increased the population of Newark to 200 by 1880.

Railroad-related industries were the first to locate in Newark. The Carter Brothers Car Foundry and Manufacturing Works was joined in 1882 by James Graham's iron foundry and in 1883 by C.P. Ingraham's brass foundry. The town had hotels, a general store, an ornate railroad depot, a central park, a school, and, for a short time, a newspaper, the *Enterprise.*

In 1887 Fair leased the railroad to the Central Pacific. Loss of the railroad headquarters was an economic disaster for Newark.

EDEN TOWNSHIP

Eden Township includes Ranchos San Leandro and San Lorenzo, and part of Rancho San Antonio. Some of Alameda County's most turbulent land disputes took place here.

By the early 1850s the land along San Leandro Creek had been usurped by so many squatters that Squattersville (now San Lorenzo) was considered one of the three towns in Contra Costa County. Some of the intruders fenced the Estudillo stock away from the creek and shot the family's horses and cattle. Fearing for their safety, the Estudillos deeded some of the property to Clement Boyreau, an alien, to bring suit in federal court.

William Heath Davis (perhaps best known as the author of Sixty Years in California) came to Alameda County (then Contra Costa) in the 1840s. In November 1847 he married Maria Estudillo, daughter of Don José Joaquin Estudillo, the owner of Rancho San Leandro. Davis settled in present-day San Leandro and laid out much of the community. Courtesy, San Leandro Community Library Center

The decision favored the Estudillos, and the squatters took leases from the family pending review by the U.S. Supreme Court. Ultimately the squatters had to pay for the land.

The town of San Leandro was plotted in the mid-1850s by John B. Ward and William Heath Davis, sons-in-law of José Joaquin Estudillo, who managed the property after his death in 1852. As the center of population moved northward, the public pressured the county government to move to a more central location. In 1855, after the Estudillo family offered to provide land for a new courthouse, the court of sessions (precursor to the board of supervisors) moved to San Leandro. With the construction of the courthouse, the Estudillo House and several other hotels, and the publication of the weekly *Alameda County Gazette,* San Leandro became the focus of much social and political activity.

The influx of settlers in the San Leandro-San Lorenzo area led to the further breakup of large land holdings. The new residents, many of them Portuguese sailors from the Azores, started orchards and truck gardens. Crops ranged from the locally developed Bing cherry to seeds to sugar beets. Eden Township was best known for its orchards, however, which extended from Castro Valley almost to the bay. Firms such as the Central Manufacturing Company and Baker and Hamilton Agricul-

Above: Alameda County's courthouse in San Leandro was nearly finished and in partial use in 1868 when this picture was taken, before it was destroyed in the great earthquake of October 21. Deputy County Clerk J.W. Joselyn was killed when the building collapsed. Under Sheriff J.W. Borein escaped through a window and led five prisoners to safety. Courtesy, California Section, California State Library

Right: The severe temblor at 6 a.m. October 21, 1868, known by some historians as "the Great San Francisco Earthquake" until the more famous event in 1906, actually occurred along the Hayward Fault in central Alameda County. This warehouse near the Central Pacific Depot suffered major damage. The county offices in San Leandro were put out of commission, which led to their transfer to Oakland. Courtesy, Rural Alameda County Collection, California State University, Hayward

tural Works came to San Leandro to take advantage of the need for improved agricultural machinery.

Among the community's most prominent citizens was Daniel Best, who bought the San Leandro Plow Company in 1886. Best introduced several innovations to the area, including a steam traction harvester and thresher and a gasoline automobile. He built a business block and a theater, and became a civic leader and a principal in the First National Bank of San Leandro.

The town of Hayward had its beginnings

in 1851 when William Hayward bought 40 acres of Rancho San Lorenzo from Guillermo Castro. Hayward started a store, a dairy, and a hotel/tavern that quickly became a renowned resort. As road commissioner for Alameda County, Hayward built roads connecting his hotel with Mt. Eden, Alvarado, Dublin, and Squattersville. Castro plotted the town in 1854, and sold the rest of his property 10 years later.

The area was devastated by the earthquake of 1868. Two people were killed; numerous buildings were knocked off their foundations or overturned; and an open crack in the ground, three or four inches wide, extended along the foothills from Hayward to Niles.

Mt. Eden probably dates to the building of Eden's Landing in 1850. J.L. Shiman built the first village houses and store there; he soon had a competitor, Edward Clawiter. Eric Ruus built the Danish Hotel, and in 1883 Henry Peterson, Jr., built the Wigwam auditorium at Hesperian Boulevard and Jackson. With a fine stage and a capacity of 400, the Wigwam served as a center for community gatherings for many years.

Castro Valley was developed largely by James Harvey Strobridge. He came to the area to construct the Southern Pacific line from Niles to Oakland but stayed to raise crops and cattle and to breed horses.

The farmers of Eden Township soon began to export their crops beyond the local market. In 1867 Daniel Perkins exhibited 130 varieties of seed at the Paris Exhibition, and thereafter received orders from Europe and Asia. Orchardists shipped their fresh fruits packed in ice to New York or had them dried by the Hayward Fruit Growers' Association or Russell and Kimball. By the early 1900s the Hayward area had some of the world's largest shippers of green peas, rhubarb, apricots, and tomatoes.

MURRAY TOWNSHIP

East of Eden is Murray Township, defined as "embracing all the territory not included in the townships before specified . . ." The area includes three ranchos: José Maria Amador's San Ramon, Robert Livermore's Los Positas, and El Valle de San Jose, originally deeded to the Bernals, Sunols, and Picos. John W. Kottinger married a daughter of Juan P. Bernal in 1850 and built his home at Alisal in 1852. In 1863 Joshua Ayres Neal and his wife, a daughter of Agustín Bernal, established residence nearby, and the two families had their lands surveyed in order to sell lots. They named the town Pleasanton after Alfred Pleasonton, commander of the Cavalry Corps of the Army of the Potomac.

In the early years Pleasanton was notorious as a haven for gamblers and desperados. Joaquin Murietta is said to have escaped detection in Pleasanton by hiding under a woman's hoopskirt as the sheriff searched her house.

Pleasanton was also famous for its racetrack, laid out in 1858 by Agustín Bernal's sons. The track, augmented by stable facilities, gained such a positive reputation that many wealthy Easterners sent their racehorses to Pleasanton for winter training. The community became a center for horse breeding, and Pleasanton hay was sold as far afield as England. Among the oldest racetracks in the United States, the oval is still in use at the Alameda County Fairgrounds.

Another community landmark is La Hacienda del Pozo de Verona, the showplace built by Phoebe Apperson Hearst in 1904. An internationally known philanthropist and an unex-

celled hostess, Hearst entertained here on a level that provided income to the community equivalent to that from a large factory.

Livermore had its beginnings in 1855, when Alphonso Ladd built a hotel near Robert Livermore's home and named the settlement Laddville. In 1868 William Mendenhall donated 20 acres of his land west of Laddville for a railroad depot. He then had his adjacent property surveyed and laid out a community that he named Livermore, in honor of his friend.

Livermore was incorporated in 1876 with a population of 830 and a flour mill, blacksmith shops, a brewery, grain warehouses, hotels, saloons, harness makers, a firehouse, a newspaper, and a college. Viticulture became important in the Livermore Valley, and by 1885 more than 4,000 acres were planted in grapes. Carl Wente, a German, founded his winery in 1883, and James Concannon came from Ireland to establish the winery that still bears his name.

Dublin was started by Michael Murray and Jeremiah Fallon, natives of Ireland who came west together in 1846. In 1852 they bought a part of Rancho San Ramon from José Maria Amador. Murray and Fallon were joined in 1857 by John Green, who became storekeeper, postmaster, and supervisor for Murray Township. (The township is named for Murray, who was the district's first county supervisor.) Since he spoke Spanish and had studied land tenure laws, Green was counted a friend and an adviser by the Mexican grantees. James Witt

La Hacienda del Pozo del Verona, now the Castlewood Country Club near Pleasanton, was originally the home of Phoebe Apperson Hearst. Architect Julia Morgan designed the Mediterranean-style villa. This photo is of the original Hacienda, which was damaged by fire in 1969. The villa was rebuilt to serve as the country club. Courtesy, Amador-Livermore Valley Historical Society

The Carl Wente family posed for this photograph in 1890. Wente arrived in the Livermore Valley in 1883 from Germany and established his winery, using vine cuttings from his native land. Courtesy, Amador-Livermore Valley Historical Society

Dougherty bought much of the Amador grant in 1852, and the area was known as Dougherty's Station for several years.

THE NORTH COUNTY

The magnificent stand of redwoods atop the Oakland-Berkeley Hills was first noted on a map prepared by Juan Manuel de Ayala, commander of the first vessel to survey the bay in 1775. Settlers later described the trees as immense; the largest was said to be 32 feet in diameter and 300 feet tall. For 75 years the tallest trees served as navigational landmarks to sea captains entering the Golden Gate.

There were three main groves: the San Antonio along the crest of the hills, the Middle along Redwood Creek, and the Moraga above San Leandro Creek. All lay within the adjoining lands granted to Luis Peralta (Rancho San Antonio) and Joaquin Moraga (Rancho Laguna de los Palos Colorados). The original beams and timbers of Mission San Jose were hewn in these forests, and when the ranchos were granted, the padres retained cutting rights. A portion of the forest between the two ranchos was later set aside as public land.

Between 1840 and 1842 several groups

of ship deserters began cutting lumber for sale. Beginning in 1846 men like William A. Leidesdorff and Harry Meiggs started commercial logging on a large scale. By 1849 a small steam sawmill had been built on Palo Seco Creek, above Dimond Canyon, and there were approximately 100 loggers at work in the forests. By 1853 the number had increased to between 300 and 400—larger than the population of any East Bay town. When San Francisco exploded from 800 to 42,000 people, the demand for lumber, and the price, skyrocketed. By 1855 the forests were virtually gone, stripped to build and rebuild San Francisco, which by 1851 had been destroyed six times by fire.

The burgeoning town needed food as well as housing, and hunters shot any game in sight, including Spanish cattle. Rancho San Antonio lost about $100,000 a year in cattle just before the sale of the land became unavoidable.

Not far behind the hunters came farmers who wanted to raise produce for the San Francisco market. Within a few months the Peralta lands were literally overrun. Although the Peraltas received confirmation of their land grants in 1854, the case was not settled until 1885, and by that time the decision was moot.

BERKELEY

In the fall of 1853 Domingo Peralta sold 40 acres at the foot of Gilman Street to a San Francisco meat-market proprietor, John J. Fleming. A few weeks later the beleaguered ranchero sold the rest of his land for $82,000, reserving only 300 acres around his home. This was a fortune in those days, but Peralta owed most of the money to lawyers, tax collectors, and others from whom he had borrowed to pursue his claim.

The four purchasers were Hall McAllister, Lucien Hermann, R.P. Hammond, and Joseph K. Irving. Irving died suddenly after mortgaging his share to a Missouri banking firm, which then offered presumably valid titles to purchasers. In this way Francis Kittredge Shattuck, William Hillegass, George M. Blake, and James Leonard joined the pioneer landowners of Berkeley, as did former squatters Michael Curtis and Henry Erskine Carleton.

ALBANY

In 1853 Captain James H. Jacobs built a house and a wharf for his freight sloop near the mouth of Strawberry Creek. Jacobs' Landing, along with the inn and grocery store opened in 1854 by William J. Bowen, attracted industry along the Contra Costa Road. The Pioneer Starch and Grist Mill, opened in 1855 by John Everding and A. Rammelsburg, prospered for nearly a century.

Zimri Brewer Heywood developed a substantial wharf for the sale and transshipment of lumber at Jacobs' Landing. When the Board of Tidelands Commissioners was established in 1868 to "survey and dispose of certain salt marsh and tide lands," Heywood and Jacobs were allowed to acquire title to their properties for payment of "amounts varying from $1.50 to $23 per acre, depending on how wet one's feet got in pacing off each acre." A portion of this settlement merged with Berkeley in 1878. The balance of the community was incorporated as Ocean View in 1908 and the name changed to Albany in 1909.

EMERYVILLE

One of the largest Indian shell mounds was located at the mouth of Temescal Creek on land owned by Vicénte Peralta. Edward Wiard bought this property in 1859. He leveled the eastern cone to construct the Oakland Trotting Park by 1871 and later converted the western cone into Shellmound Park, a huge resort and picnic grounds that attracted pleasure seekers from the entire Bay Area until its closure in 1924.

The area was known as Golden Gate Village until 1896, when it was renamed in honor of an early resident, Joseph Stickney Emery. The California Jockey Club operated the track until gambling was outlawed in 1911. Industrial firms quickly purchased the large parcels of land near two railroads, and Emeryville became a blue-collar community.

PIEDMONT

Sometime before 1852 Vicénte Peralta sold

"all the dry land north of San Antonio Creek and west of San Antonio Slough [Lake Merritt]" to a group of speculators including Colonel John C. Hayes, who built his home in the wooded hills behind the present city of Piedmont. Here he entertained such visitors as John C. Frémont, who is said to have christened the Golden Gate while watching the sunset from Hayes' garden.

Other early residents included Walter and William Blair, who started a farm, dairy, and nursery for eucalyptus seedlings on 600 acres bought from the U.S. government for $1.25 an acre. In 1876 the brothers constructed a horse-car line from Seventh and Broadway in Oakland to Piedmont Avenue and then north to the entrance of the Mountain View Cemetery.

The discovery of white sulfur springs led to the development of a popular resort centered around the Piedmont Springs Hotel, and soon wealthy San Francisco businessmen were building personal estates in the area. Among the most prominent was the home of the Isaac L. Requa family, which was said to be a duplicate of the governor's mansion in Sacramento.

With the inauguration of the short-lived Piedmont Cable Car Line in 1890, horsecars were replaced with cable cars and new subdivisions proliferated. William Dingee, Arthur H. Breed, Sr., and other developers held a gala picnic and auction to sell the first lots in the Dingee tract. Residents incorporated the City of Piedmont on January 30, 1907.

ALAMEDA

In 1851 Antonio Peralta sold the entire Alameda peninsula for $14,000 to Gideon Aughinbaugh and William Chipman, who laid out a subdivision of four-acre lots selling for $80 apiece. To encourage settlement from San Francisco they established a ferry route and at one time offered a free lot to anyone who would build a house on it. In April 1854 Alameda was incorporated as a town with 154 residents, but because the townspeople neglected to elect any officers the incorporation was voided and the process had to be repeated in 1872.

Alameda developed as a residential area,

Piedmont Park featured a maze of hedges as its centerpiece in 1896. Courtesy, Amador-Livermore Valley Historical Society

although agriculture was also important in the early years. Orchards, vegetables, clover, and grains throve on the peninsula, and dairies dotted the township.

A.A. Cohen, whose San Francisco and Alameda Railroad provided commuter service in connection with ferries to San Francisco in 1863, soon extended the line to Hayward. By 1869, when the Western Pacific Railroad line was completed to the Alameda Wharf, land values for the town had risen from $300,000 to more than $4,000,000.

During the 1870s and 1880s the oyster beds along the south shore were harvested by the Pacific Oyster Company. Other industries included an oil refinery, a soap company, breweries, pottery works, and factories producing carriages, nails, and asphaltum pipe.

In 1874 the federal government began to dredge San Antonio Creek and the bar, and three years later oceangoing vessels could anchor on the Alameda side of the estuary. The peninsula became an island in 1902 when the army engineers opened the Tidal Canal. These harbor improvements, combined with the location of the transcontinental railroad terminus at the Oakland Mole, made the Oakland-Alameda harbor competitive with Vallejo and in time with San Francisco.

BROOKLYN

Moses Chase came to the Contra Costa in

1849 to hunt wild game for the San Francisco market. He fell ill and was nursed back to health by the Patten brothers, Robert, Edwin, and William. The Pattens had secured a lease of 150 acres on the east side of San Antonio Slough (Lake Merritt) from Antonio Peralta, and they asked Chase to join them in a farming venture. The partners eventually bought additional property and began to lay out a town.

Chase returned to Massachusetts to marry his fiancée, Mary Ellen Clinton, only to find that she had died during his absence. He named the new settlement Clinton in her memory.

Meanwhile James B. Larue started a store and built a wharf at the foot of what is now 13th Avenue. This developed into the settlement of San Antonio. In 1856 the two towns were consolidated under the name Brooklyn at the suggestion of one of the supervisors, Thomas Eager, who had arrived on the ship of that name in 1846. A third village, formed to the northeast of Clinton in 1867, was named after Lynn, Massachusetts, because both towns had shoe factories. These three settlements merged into the town of Brooklyn when it was incorporated in 1870. Two years later Brooklyn was annexed by Oakland.

OAKLAND

Edson Adams, Andrew J. Moon, and Horace W. Carpentier arrived on the Contra Costa in 1850. After a squatting incident which included a writ of ejectment served on them by the Contra Costa County sheriff, the trio secured leases of 160 acres apiece from Vicénte Peralta. They hired Julius Kellenberger to survey their three adjacent plots and lay out streets, and began selling lots they did not own. Alfred W. Burrell, who arrived in 1851, was given property in return for building a hotel.

Carpentier, a lawyer, immediately set out to develop the port. On August 1, 1851, he and Moon obtained a franchise from the county to operate a daily ferry service to San Francisco, with fees ranging from 50 cents per hundredweight for freight to five dollars for a wagon with two horses.

Next, becoming involved with the state legislature, he secured passage of a bill incorpo-

Left: The three founders of Oakland, Horace W. Carpentier, Edson Adams, and Andrew Moon (left to right), arrived on the Contra Costa in 1850. They immediately recognized the suitability of the wooded site along the estuary for a great city, and the potential profits for those who would develop it. Courtesy, Oakland History Room, Oakland Public Library

Below: Completion of the Oakland Tidal Canal in 1902 linked San Antonio Creek with San Leandro Bay and consequently made the city of Alameda an island. Plans had been laid as early as 1873, but Congressional and local opposition forced repeated delays in the project. Courtesy, Oakland History Room, Oakland Public Library

rating the Town of Oakland on May 4, 1852. Mariano Vallejo is said to have suggested the name, which is derived from the previous Spanish place-name Encinal, or Oak Grove.

Members of the first board of trustees were Amédée Marier (the postmaster), A.W. Burrell, Moon, Adams, and Carpentier, who soon withdrew. Within two weeks the board approved an ordinance conveying the Oakland waterfront to Carpentier in exchange for his constructing three wharves and a school. Although the ordinance had limited Carpentier's control of the waterfront to 37 years, in August 1853, with completion of his construction obligation, the board granted Carpentier the waterfront "in fee simple forever." Local citizens challenged the action by attempting to oust the three trustees in an election. When that failed riots broke out, but to no avail.

Meanwhile Carpentier busied himself with yet another civic improvement. To go from Oakland to Clinton and San Antonio, one had to row a boat across San Antonio Slough (Lake Merritt) or go around it on foot, on horseback, or by carriage. The county supervisors contracted with T.C. Gilman to build a bridge for $7,400 at about the location of the later 12th Street Dam. When the county was unable to pay, Carpentier offered financial backing in return for permission to operate the crossing as a toll bridge.

In a hotly disputed election in March 1853, Carpentier won a seat representing Contra Costa County in the state assembly. He joined Henry C. Smith of Santa Clara County in a move to establish a new county, Alameda, with Oakland as the county seat. Carpentier suffered one of his few setbacks when the functions of county government were divided between New Haven and Alvarado. When Oakland was incorporated as a city in 1854, he became the first mayor.

The earthquake of 1868 triggered the removal of the county seat to Oakland. The county courthouse in San Leandro collapsed and losses were severe. After much discussion, Brooklyn became the county seat in 1873. But Oakland had already annexed Brooklyn, and Carpentier's city became the county's seat of government.

The Oakland, San Leandro and Haywards Electric Railway provided the fastest transportation available for the East Bay coastal communities in the 1890s and early 1900s. Courtesy, Oakland History Room, Oakland Public Library

CHAPTER 3

MACHINES AND METAL RIBBONS

As Alameda County's communities grew and prospered, the need for more effective transportation increased. While stage service along the Contra Costa began at an early date, the roads were bumpy and often impassable during the rainy season. The only practical way to reach San Francisco was by water.

Commercial water transport began even before the Gold Rush, as the sloop *Pirouette* carried passengers and goods from the San Antonio wharf to San Francisco, returning with imported manufactured supplies. Beginning in 1850 the propeller steamer *Kangaroo* made the trip across the bay twice a week, carrying mostly work crews and lumber from the redwoods. The steamer *Union* began daily trips from Alameda Creek in 1851. That same year Horace W. Carpentier and Charles Minturn instituted daily ferry service from Oakland to San Francisco; Captain James H. Jacob's sloop connected San Francisco with the Contra Costa road in 1853. Many people made the trip in whaleboats or small sailing vessels, but unfavorable winds could maroon a boat on the extensive mudflats for several hours until the next high tide.

WOOING THE RAILROAD

Alameda County felt especially isolated from the Eastern United States during the 1850s. As early as 1845 Congress had entertained a proposal for a transcontinental railroad, which would cut travel time between the coasts from six weeks to six days. But lawmakers had done nothing to promote the project. The Democratic Party, the dominant political force during this period, was thus associated with inaction on the railroad issue.

Consequently, when John C. Frémont ran as the Republican candidate in the 1856 presidential election, Alameda County supported him. While he polled third place in California, the significance of this election is in the Republican affiliation of several influential individuals: Collis P. Huntington, Mark Hopkins, Charles Crocker, and Leland Stanford, later to become known as the "Big Four" of the Central Pacific Railroad. Huntington and Hopkins were delegates to the national Republican convention, whose platform guaranteed that California would get a railroad if their party was elected.

As tension between the North and the South increased, ramifications were felt locally. In 1859 Stanford was chosen the Republican gubernatorial candidate, but the pro-slavery Democrats defeated him. In 1860 Alameda was one of the few California counties that supported the Republican cause by voting for Abraham Lincoln. Running again as the Republican candidate in 1861, Stanford was elected governor.

Such was the state of affairs when Theodore H. Judah, an engineer with a dream of a railroad spanning the continent, began raising money to accomplish that feat. Failing to garner sufficient funds in the Bay Area, he convinced a group of Sacramento businessmen to

Right: As they did throughout the West, Chinese immigrants provided Alameda County railroads a cheap source of labor for construction. From Leslie's Magazine, *1876, from the Bancroft Library. Courtesy, Oakland Museum, History Department*

Below: Dr. Samuel Merritt (rear) and his guests are pictured here on his yacht Casco circa 1888. The Oakland physician/mayor outfitted the ship with Belgian rugs, chandeliers, and other items of Victorian luxury. Author Robert Louis Stevenson chartered the Casco in June 1888 for his voyage described in In the South Seas. *Historians have debated over whether the man at the far right is or isn't Stevenson. Courtesy, Oakland History Room, Oakland Public Library*

support his venture. The Central Pacific Railroad Company of California was incorporated with Stanford as president, Huntington as vice-president, Hopkins as treasurer, and Crocker as one of the directors. Judah received federal financial assistance in 1862 when Congress and President Lincoln approved a bill aiding the construction of a transcontinental railroad, with the Western portion of the line to be built by the Central Pacific.

With Judah's death in 1863 the Big Four soon controlled the company and amassed a fortune in federal grants for their project. Construction of the line was under the direction of Crocker, who determined to utilize Chinese labor. By the end of the project more than 40,000 Chinese men were working on Western railroads. Their presence would affect the future of all of California.

The Central Pacific had begun in Sacramento on its trek east, but needed ties to the Bay Area. Oakland was ultimately selected for this important terminal. Alameda County's Republican support had paid off! Dr. Samuel Merritt, who became mayor of Oakland in 1867, was a key individual in this decision. Working with both the Big Four and

Carpentier, he negotiated the formation of a new political entity, the Oakland Waterfront Company.

As president of the Oakland Waterfront Company and a director of the Central Pacific, Carpentier deeded all his waterfront lands to the new concern. The Oakland City Council, through Merritt's intervention, abandoned all legal claims to the waterfront. The Oakland Waterfront Company then sold 500 acres of its new holdings to Central Pacific's subsidiary, the Western Pacific. Oakland had its railroad, and the Central Pacific its essential Western terminus. Shortly after that Carpentier went back to his native New York State, where he resided until his death in 1918 at the age of 93.

In May 1869 the Central Pacific met the Union Pacific at Promontory Point, Utah. In September the first transcontinental train reached San Francisco Bay. It had to be routed to the Alameda Wharf, as the Western Pacific had not yet completed the Oakland pier. Once Oakland's dock was finished, ferryboats operated by the Central Pacific met the trains so that both commerce and passengers could continue to San Francisco.

The subsidies granted by the federal government allowed the Central Pacific to gain monopolistic control over railroading in California, as it bought out smaller companies and consolidated them into the Southern Pacific Railroad Company.

THE END OF ISOLATION

The coming of the railroad changed the face of Alameda County. Along the right-of-way,

hamlets grew into towns almost overnight. Oakland, the terminus, became a full-fledged city.

New facilities were needed to keep pace with the growing population. Anthony Chabot and T.W. Boardman formed the Contra Costa Water Company in the late 1860s to provide Oakland and environs a water supply by damming various creeks to create Lake Temescal and Lake Chabot. In the 1890s the Piedmont Water Company extended competing lines into Oakland, drilling wells at Alvarado to increase its supply. The two companies finally merged.

During this same period Oakland hastened to provide street paving, gasworks, sewer lines, streetlights, a subscription library, and, by 1880, a telephone system. The estuary of San Antonio Slough was dammed to create Lake Merritt, the nation's oldest officially designated wildlife preserve.

Above: The Oakland Terminal of the Central Pacific Railroad is shown here in 1885. The structure covered an area of over four acres. The central portion received overland trains, while the side sections handled local traffic and connected with ferry steamers to San Francisco. Courtesy, Berkeley Historical Society

Below: The first terminus of the transcontinental railroad was located at the foot of Pacific Street in Alameda. The first train arrived in September 1869. Two months later the terminus was switched to Seventh and Broadway in Oakland. Courtesy, Oakland History Room, Oakland Public Library

In 1863, having outgrown two previous locations, Oakland bought 200 acres of land outside the city limits and established Mountain View Cemetery. Catholic and Jewish groups bought adjacent land for burial grounds. Health care was improved in 1860 when a group of physicians formed the Alameda County Medical Society. In 1876, 18 women gave $50 apiece and uncounted hours of volunteer service to establish the Oakland Homeopathic Hospital and Dispensary (later Fabiola Hospital).

Meanwhile metal ribbons began crisscrossing Alameda County as the California legislature authorized the construction of local railroad lines. The San Francisco and Oakland Railroad Company, running from Broadway to the bay, was completed in 1863 and two years later linked up with the San Francisco and Alameda Railroad, which extended from the Alameda Wharf to Hayward. The Oakland Railroad Company built tracks to accommodate horsecars and steam trains. The Western Pacific was organized in 1862 to build a line from Sacramento to San Jose with a branch line to Oakland. It soon became a subsidiary of the Central Pacific.

The Oakland Gas, Light, and Heat Company began providing electrical service in 1885, and the first Oakland home was electrically lit in 1891. In 1902 the Suburban Electric Company supplied home lighting to 1,500 residences in Oakland, Hayward, and San Leandro. However until 1891 the use of electricity for railroads was deemed unconstitutional. Af-

ter several petitions from Alameda County, the state legislature passed legislation that permitted railroad electrification. The Oakland and Berkeley Transit Company, the Sessions-Vandercook Line, the Southern Pacific, and the Oakland, San Leandro and Haywards Electric Railroad were among those operating at the turn of the century.

During these years Oakland traction magnate Francis M. "Borax" Smith began developing and consolidating a profitable network of interurban electric railways. In 1902 his Oakland Transit Company took over control of its only independent competitor, the Oakland, San Leandro and Haywards Electric Railroad. In 1903 Smith opened a line to Berkeley and linked it to San Francisco. Soon all of Oakland, Berkeley, and Piedmont were linked through his "Key Route" train and ferry system. The Southern Pacific Company suddenly found it had a competitor in the East Bay whose transportation system was considerably faster, with more service, than Southern Pacific's.

Spurred by the ease of transportation and the industrial growth related to the railroads, the population of Oakland exploded from 1,543 in 1860 to 34,555 in 1886, and to 65,000 by the turn of the century. Iron works, soap works, marble works, and breweries provided jobs to the new residents. Carriages were made by concerns like the Pioneer Carriage Company, the Western Carriage Company, and the Oakland Carriage Factory. Lumber production intensified and planing mills felt the increased demand generated by the new, more intricate styles of architectural trim. Alameda County's agricultural abundance was reflected in canneries, flour mills, and textile mills; in fact Oakland had the only cotton mills west of Chicago.

The railroads brought to Oakland a well-educated population of blacks who worked as porters and hotel employees. Oakland became one of the first cities in California to admit blacks to the public schools. In 1874 the Reverend Jeremiah Sanderson formed the Equal Rights League to promote the civil rights of blacks in Alameda County. The 1900 Oakland city directory lists 1,000 black residences, three newspapers, a retirement home, two churches, and numerous businesses, clubs, lodges, and

Key Route electric trains connected with Key Route ferries via the long pier from 1903 to 1939. The Bay Bridge closely followed this route toward Yerba Buena Island in the distance. Courtesy, Oakland History Room, Oakland Public Library

Men in rural Alameda County gathered in local saloons in the early days. Hayward's Py's Corner patrons played euchre for rounds of drinks in 1901. The saloon was torn down in 1928 to make room for a filling station. Courtesy, Rural Alameda County Collection, California State University, Hayward

other organizations. By the early 20th century the black population was increasing dramatically, attracted by an increasing number of jobs in the area.

Completion of the railroad glutted California's markets. At the same time, unemployment soared as the railroad discharged thousands of unskilled workers. The Chinese found employment building dams, sea walls, and harbor improvements; they worked in the cigar, ceramics, and explosives factories, in the shipyards and the cotton mill; they entered domestic service as houseboys, cooks, and gardeners; they worked as sharecroppers; they sold fruits and vegetables door to door; and they gained a near-monopoly on the laundry business.

POLITICAL MACHINES AT WORK

In 1873 a financial panic occurred, followed by a depression. Henry George, editor of the Oakland *Transit,* published several articles urging reforms that would limit the railroad's profits from land speculation. But the Big Four's monopoly overshadowed every other Alameda County business, and its workers could ill afford to express political opposition to their company. Consequently resentment was directed against blacks and the Chinese.

On October 5, 1877, Denis Kearney formed the Workingmen's Party of California.

Its platform included ridding the country of cheap Chinese labor, destroying the land monopoly of the railroad, organizing against the "dangerous encroachments of capital," and demanding such "radical" reforms as an eight-hour day, direct election of senators, compulsory education, and a more equitable system of taxation. On November 10, 1877, some 10,000 workers including a delegation from Oakland marched in a parade in San Francisco.

The Workingmen's Party won its first victory when John Bones was elected to fill the seat left vacant by the death of Alameda County's Republican senator, Nathan Porter. The party also helped elect Oakland's Mayor Washington Andrus, the city attorney, a judge, and two council members, and carried elections in Hayward, San Leandro, and Berkeley.

Concurrently a convention was held to formulate a new state constitution. Although the Workingmen had a strong delegation, Republicans and Democrats banded together to counter the new party's strength. The result was a constitution of compromises that included an elected railroad commission, an anti-Chinese article, and a longer school year, but no reforms that would lead to resolution of the state's serious social and economic issues. With the passage of the new constitution, the power of the Workingmen's Party began to decline.

During this period Rutherford B. Hayes became the first president to visit California

Right: Chinese "basket brigades" were virtually the sole suppliers of fresh produce in the East Bay until the late 1870s. Chinese farmers in the East Bay sold their crops to San Francisco merchants who then dispatched their Chinese salesmen back across the bay. Courtesy, Oakland History Room, Oakland Public Library

Facing page, top: This early 1900s view of lower Oakland was taken from the roof of the former county courthouse at Fourth and Broadway. Courtesy, California Section, California State Library

Below: In this 1916 photo, pears ripened on the trees while the Wigines farm raised summer crops between the rows of the orchard. The practice of intercropping, introduced to Alameda County by the Chinese, was among the agricultural techniques later used in other California counties. Courtesy, California State Archives

while in office. His wife was entertained in Oakland by the city's social elite.

The 1880s were marked by general prosperity following the turbulence of the previous decade. However a degree of political instability occurred as neither party could quite fill the social reform void vacated by the Workingmen. Scandals in the California legislature caused statewide indignation which paved the way for a new party.

The Populist Party stood for government ownership of transportation, an eight-hour day

on public works projects, women's suffrage, and the outlawing of saloons. Although the party failed to win a senatorial seat in the 1892 election, the Populists elected eight assemblymen including Arnold Bretz of Oakland. The votes of the "Big Eight" were needed to obtain a majority in a legislature composed of 59 Democrats and 51 Republicans.

During 1893 another panic occurred again followed by a depression. Once more the railroad was the target of animosity. During the famous Pullman Strike, Oakland's local railroad workers struck also. Originally only Pullman cars were not to be handled; other railroad operations were to continue as usual. However the Southern Pacific fired those who would not move the Pullman coaches. Soon the unrest spread with strikers preventing train operations at Oakland's railroad yards. In July 1894 the first federal injunction in United States history was issued against strikers, and the strike was soon broken.

One outcome of the strike was the sentiment that the Populist Party could become a major political power in California. All three parties, however, embraced the anti-railroad sentiment in 1894, which diffused Populist support. The Republicans scored a landslide victory, and by 1898 the Populists had lost their influence.

During the same period the Southern Pacific had attained so much power that it formed a political bureau. Concurrently, anti-Southern Pacific political advocates grew powerful in their own right. In 1898 Republicans supported the gubernatorial aspirations of George C. Pardee, who had been Oakland's mayor from 1893-1895, but the Southern Pacific's choice, Henry Gage, won the election.

Four years later, realizing that Gage would be defeated if supporters of the two opposition candidates combined forces, the Southern Pacific threw its support to the candidate it considered least threatening. With the unwavering support of his Alameda County contingent, George C. Pardee of Oakland became governor of California.

Pardee's administration is noted for supporting a state highway system, urging adoption of a direct primary, and supporting conservation. He should have been a prime candidate for reelection, but delegates who re-

sented the Southern Pacific's support of his 1902 candidacy joined with the Southern Pacific in nominating James Gillett, who became governor in 1906.

THE EARTH SHOOK

That year ushered in more than a political upset for Alameda County, however. The April 1906 earthquake was the most destructive in the recorded history of the Bay Area. Alameda County's communities sustained major damage. In Livermore virtually half of all the town's structures received some damage, and in San Leandro almost every building needed repairs. The destruction in Oakland was enormous, overshadowing the rest of the East Bay.

Even with all that, the damage in Alameda County did not reach the destructive proportions of that in San Francisco. Thousands of refugees fled to the East Bay. The Southern Pacific provided not only relief materials but also free transportation across the bay. Oakland alone cared for more than 100,000 people, while Berkeley, Alameda, San Leandro, Newark, and Hayward housed thousands more. Camps were set up wherever possible and every available public building was used to shelter the homeless survivors. Even San Francisco's newspapers were published and printed in Oakland.

Oakland, Berkeley, and Alameda bustled in the earthquake's aftermath, with real estate promoters lauding the East Bay as a safe place to live. Many did relocate during this period, and real estate prices skyrocketed. The events of 1906 forced modernization that otherwise would have been long in coming.

Alameda County was formed and its settlement pattern dictated by 19th-century events, but its true proportions, intense growth, and the full scope of its importance would follow its entry into the modern era after 1906.

Above: The Great San Francisco Earthquake of 1906 devastated parts of Alameda County. Brick structures such as the Gallegos Winery (shown) near Mission San Jose and the nearby Southern Pacific shipping warehouse fell victim to the temblor. Courtesy, Washington Township Historical Society

In 1918 "the Campanile," or the Sather Tower, dominated the University of California, Berkeley, campus. Despite the addition of numerous high-rise structures, it continues as the university's focal point today. Jane K. Sather donated $225,000 for construction of the tower and its 12 original bells. Courtesy, Oakland Museum, History Department

REACHING IN AND REACHING OUT

Alameda County has long been recognized as a leading educational and intellectual center of the West, attracting students and faculty from around the globe.

There was an early recognition in California of the need to forge an American culture out of the panoply of peoples attracted by the Gold Rush; the constitution of 1850 mandated the establishment of a state university. But it was the religious community that took the lead in establishing schools at all levels.

The Reverend Samuel Hopkins Willey, sent to California by the American Home Missionary Society in 1848, first taught school in Monterey while acting as chaplain for the Constitutional Convention. Working with the Reverends Joseph A. Benton and Samuel Blakeslee, he explored ways to start a preparatory academy and also a college. In 1851, as pastor of Howard Presbyterian Church in San Francisco, he led a parade of 100 children down Montgomery Street to dramatize the need for public schools in that city. With the arrival of the Reverend Henry Durant in 1853 they found their first schoolmaster. Willey had already chosen Oakland, then one year old, as the ideal site. On June 20, 1853, the Contra Costa Academy opened with three pupils. By 1859 the academy was preparing 70 students to enter the hoped-for College of California.

The committee's application for a college charter was granted in 1855, but it was 1860 before the college opened in a small building on the grounds of the academy. The Reverend Isaac H. Brayton became the second principal of the preparatory school when Durant joined the faculty of the new college. Money continued to be a problem, as Eastern denominations believed California to be paved with gold and local congregations wanted to support their own schools rather than the nondenominational college. Brayton himself advanced funds for badly needed facilities.

The 1867 legislative decision to establish a College of Agriculture, Mining, and Mechanic Arts in Alameda County created the fear that the federal subsidy provided through the Morrill Land Grant Act of 1862 would become available only for technical training and not the liberal arts. Realizing that the College of California, as a private institution, was ineligible for government funding, the trustees arranged an advantageous merger. By transferring title to the college's lands, buildings, equipment, and library to the state, they guaranteed the inclusion of its classical curriculum in the new University of California.

DEVELOPING A CAMPUS AND A FACULTY

The college had earlier purchased 160 acres of vacant land near Strawberry Creek for a future campus. After the site was dedicated in April 1860, work began to develop both the college and the community that would surround it. Landscape designer Frederick Law Olmsted assisted with plans to beautify the development. The College Homestead Association was incorporated in September 1864; lots were divided, and each purchaser of a share in the association was entitled to buy one for $550. The college trustees were so determined to promote the community that they personally purchased lots, and also started the College Water Works, which one boast credited with being able to supply the needs of Oakland as well as of the college town.

After a great deal of debate, the emerging community was named in honor of George Berkeley, bishop of Cloyne, the 18th-century philosopher and patron of education who wrote, "Westward the course of empire takes its way." The name was officially adopted in May 1866.

Henry Durant, who later served as mayor of Oakland (1873-1875), was named the first president of the university. Working with the Board of Regents, he undertook to build a faculty of stature to attract able students. The first professors to be hired were John and Joseph LeConte, both of whom had medical degrees from the College of Physicians and Surgeons in New York and previous experience on the faculties of well-known Eastern universities. Coming to California as the core of the new faculty, they were to serve the university with distinction for 25 years. John LeConte, who taught physics, was also the president of the university from 1876-1881, while Joseph became involved in the conservation movement in Yosemite and taught until his retirement in 1896.

The LeContes were joined by William Weicher, like the LeContes, a Confederate army veteran. After being denied the university presidency for apparently political reasons in 1881, Weicher was elected state superintendent of schools. He was later named a professor emeritus at UC.

To this growing community of intellectual endeavor were drawn some of the most remarkable, creative, and productive talents of the late 19th and early 20th centuries. Extraordinary professors like Edward Rowland Sill, the first prominent writer on the University of California faculty, were attracting students like Josiah Royce, who was destined to become one of America's great philosophers. Muckrakers Lincoln Steffens, who authored *The Shame of the Cities,* and Frank Norris, whose *The Octo-*

pus remains a classic, both studied at the university.

PHOEBE APPERSON HEARST

Even before the turn of the century, it was becoming apparent that the quality of the facilities at the new institution was lagging far behind the quality of the faculty. In 1896 Phoebe Apperson Hearst, who would become one of the school's primary benefactors, recognized the discrepancy and sponsored an international competition to design a "fitting home for the future of California . . . to put into it ideals that shall arouse and uplift the soul of man." The winning design in the competition was the work of Henri Emile Benard of Paris, and it provided a master plan for campus development for the next 50 years. The supervising architect, John Galen Howard, served the university well beyond the development of the site as the first director of its School of Architecture.

Not only did Mrs. Hearst provide financing for the design competition, she also underwrote the cost of several early buildings. In 1897 she became the first woman named to the Board of Regents, and during her tenure, which lasted until her death in 1919, she was actively involved in the institution's growth and improvement. This involvement ranged from sponsoring archaeological and anthropological research to recruiting the first female professors and endowing several professorships. She established an architectural library and personally supported such promising young architects as Bernard Maybeck, John Blakewell, and Julia Morgan. Each year she hosted a picnic day for the entire graduating class at her Pleasanton estate. At her death, Mrs. Hearst was called "the greatest woman California has ever known." Certainly a share of the greatness of the University of California is due directly to her care and generosity.

THE ATHENS OF THE PACIFIC

The University of California, which became the foundation of a nine-campus system in the 20th century, was not the only state educational institution to locate in the Berkeley area; in fact it wasn't even the first. The California School for the Deaf, Dumb and Blind was moved across the bay from San Francisco in 1867 and made a part of the public school system in 1905. In 1921 the institution was divided into separate schools for the deaf and the blind, both of which eventually moved to Fremont. One of the school's most noted graduates was the sculptor Douglas Tilden, who later returned as a teacher.

Private schools, too, contributed to the intellectual renown of Alameda County. Mills College, chartered in 1885 as a women's college, was founded earlier in Benicia as the Reverend T.C. Mills Seminary for Young Ladies and moved to Oakland in 1871. Holy Names College was established on the shores of Lake Merritt in 1868 as the Convent of Our Lady of the Sacred Heart. Saint Joseph's Academy for Boys, founded in 1880, merged with Saint Mary's College when that institution moved from San Francisco to Oakland in 1889. Washington College of Science and Industry, opened in Irvington in 1872, became Curtner's Seminary in 1896 and was closed after a fire two years later. The California College of Arts and Crafts, founded in Berkeley in 1907, soon moved to Oakland and branched out into general education. Armstrong College, founded in 1918 as the California School for Private Sec-

retaries, offers education in all aspects of business.

Other private schools and academies in Oakland included Blake Seminary, the California Military Academy (also known as McClure's), the Sackett School, and Golden Gate Academy. One section of the city became known as Academy Hill. Berkeley offered the Select School for Boys, Berkeley Gymnasium, Boone University School, and Kellogg School. The prestigious Anna Head School, founded by the ninth woman to graduate from the University of California, was located in Berkeley from 1887 to 1964, when it moved to East Oakland. So many California and Hawaii families sent their children to schools in Alameda County that the area became known as the Athens of the Pacific.

Below: Irvington's Curtner's Seminary promoted outdoor activities suitable for its feminine student body. Croquet was one of the more popular genteel pastimes. Courtesy, Washington Township Historical Society

THE POWER OF THE PEN

Beyond the campus, other writers, artists, and intellectuals formed a community of creativity that has seldom been equalled.

California's first poet laureate, Ina Coolbrith, served as Oakland's city librarian, coming from San Francisco in 1874. Born Josephine Smith, a niece of the founder of the Mormon Church, she and her mother took the mother's maiden name as a protection against anti-Mormon sentiments when they moved to California.

Encouraged by Bret Harte, Coolbrith soon earned a reputation as the leading 19th-century literary woman in the West. In addition to her poetry and her work as a librarian, this young intellectual was editor of the West's premier literary magazine, the *Overland Monthly.*

Much as Bret Harte had encouraged her, Coolbrith supported another local poet, Cincinnatus H. "Joaquin" Miller, who became known as the "Poet of the Sierras." His 300-acre estate in the Oakland hills, "The Hights," served for many years as a gathering spot for the local literati. This group may have included George Sterling and Edwin Markham, both of whom worked and lived in Alameda County during this period. Alameda County writers who have shaped American culture in more recent times include Allen Ginsberg and Jessica Mitford.

Of all the literary geniuses who graced this area none is more closely associated with the East Bay and especially with Oakland than Jack London. Born in San Francisco, he grew up in Oakland and attended high school there. During the times he was forced to withdraw from school and work he frequented the Oakland library, where Ina Coolbrith encouraged and guided his love of reading.

London gained notoriety not only from his literary skills but also from his involvement with the Socialist party. This involvement ran the gamut from being arrested for soapbox oratory in violation of a city ordinance to running unsuccessfully for mayor of Oakland on the Social Democratic Party ticket. A colorful character who moved up from the slums of Oakland to Piedmont before leaving Alameda County for the Sonoma Valley, London has been criticized for much of what he did. However he was never ignored or overlooked, and his impact locally and on the rest of the world continues.

A COMMUNITY OF INTERESTS

Celebrations of Alameda County's agricultural bounty began in 1859 with semiannual fairs in downtown Oakland. Flowers, horticulture, and art were featured in June; livestock, late crops, and farm machinery in the fall. Horseracing was held on a track at Gibbon's Point, and each fair concluded with a grand ball.

By 1905 the Canadian railroad magnate and sportsman, Rodney G. MacKenzie, had transformed the old Pleasanton racetrack into a highly desirable location for a permanent fairgrounds. A group of 15 businessmen, agriculturists, and stock raisers from all over the county formed the Alameda County Fair Association in 1912, selling stock in the venture at $100 a share and soliciting donations to finance the additional buildings and main entrance. Much of the work was done by volunteers, although Phoebe Apperson Hearst lent her garden staff, many plants, and "many beautiful and interesting antiques." No state or county funds were used.

For the grand opening on October 12, 1912, the *Oakland Tribune* reported that "the town was fittingly decorated with flags and bunting . . . a scene of unusual brilliance." Bands serenaded the arrivals of the 9 and 11 A.M. trains each day. New categories of entries included "fancywork," rag carpets, photography, mineral collections, and student demonstrations of students' work. By continually adjusting its program to the interests of its patrons, the Alameda County Fair has remained one of the outstanding such events in California.

Individual communities also enjoyed festivals featuring their productivity. San Leandro's Cherry Carnival, first held in 1909, grew to such proportions that it was a featured attraction at the 1915 Panama-Pacific International Exposition. A transplanted Englishman, Harry Rowell, reestablished the rodeo as an integral part of life in the 1920s, and presented exhibitions at the 1939 Golden Gate Exposition. Most of the 7,000 members of the National Rodeo Cowboy's Association have competed in the Hayward Arena.

Civic leaders in Oakland formed the Athenian Club in 1883 for the purpose of "according gentlemen of kindred spirits, interests and intellectual attainments the intermittent opportunity to indulge the genial hour." Under the leadership of Dr. Enoch H. Pardee, the first president, and officers William Dargie, John Lathrop, George de Golia, Dr. E.H. Woolsey, A.J. Eastland, D.P. Hughes, Wallace Everson, and Mack Webber, the club developed a program of literary, musical, and dramatic presentations at which both members and invited guests performed.

Thirteen years later a second gentlemen's social club grew out of an impromptu performance by a quartet composed of Dr. Frank Raines, Charles D. Boyce, Clarence Crowell, and Abe P. Leach, who serenaded the home of Charles A. Doyle. At Doyle's suggestion they founded the Nile Club, initially a musical group. In 1915 the two clubs combined as the Athenian-Nile Club. The name signifies "the seed ground of European civilization—neither Greece nor the Orient, but a world formed of the two."

Left: Jack London is perhaps the most widely read author of Alameda County's literary greats. London wrote several of his stories in Oakland, where he spent a great deal of time along the waterfront between his famous adventures. Courtesy, Oakland Museum, History Department

Below: Horse racing has been the state's most popular sport since the Bernal family laid out this track on their Rancho El Valle de San Jose in 1858. The facility was improved by Joseph Nevins in the 1870s and Rodney MacKenzie around the turn of the century. This 1910 photograph shows the oval as incorporated in the present Alameda County Fairgrounds. Golden Gate Fields in Albany is now the county's major track and home to Northern California's most important horse race, the California Derby, held every April. Courtesy, Oakland Museum, History Department

Participation in athletics was stimulated as the university teams won honors in intercollegiate track, baseball, and football. After beating both Stanford and Washington in their first season (1904), the Golden Bears crew went on to win an Olympic gold medal in 1928. The Berkeley Tennis Club, established adjacent to the Claremont Hotel shortly after World War I, helped produce two national championship contenders, Helen Wills (Moody) and Helen Jacobs.

THE PERFORMING ARTS

As early as 1890 amateur thespians were performing in Berkeley and Oakland under the direction of Professor Louis Dupont Style. The University Little Theater, the Berkeley Playhouse (founded in 1923 by Irving Pichel with the support of Sam Hume and Everett Glass), and Playmakers (led by Florence and Carol Aronovici and Mrs. Bartlett Heard) produced such "alumnae" as Carlton E. Morse and the "One Man's Family" cast, who hold the world's record for radio program longevity (28 years), and Gregory Peck of more recent fame. In 1941 Elizabeth Berryhill used her Little Theater training to start the Straw Hat Review, which became one of the nation's top regional theaters.

Beyond these poets and writers and performers of whom Alameda County can be justifiably proud, artists in other media were adding to the county's creative stature. Isadora

Mr. and Mrs. Vager and their daughter rode on a float participating in an annual Cherry Carnival parade in San Leandro circa 1920. Giant cherries from nearby orchards covered the vehicle. Other Alameda County communities also held annual harvest festivals named for their crops including Hayward (zucchini) and the Livermore Valley (wine grapes). Courtesy, San Leandro Community Library Center

Similar identification with the classical world was expressed in 1919 when 3,000 business and professional men of Oakland, Berkeley, Alameda, Piedmont, San Leandro, Emeryville, and Hayward contributed $20 apiece to found the Athens Athletic Club. Early officers included Norman de Vaux, Joseph R. Knowland, H.C. Capwell, Lynne Stanley, Arthur W. Moore, and Sherwood B. Swan.

The Berkeley campus, with its botanical gardens, museums, libraries, lecture halls, and competitive sports arenas, continued to provide a stimulus for the creative use of leisure time. Even though music was not included in the early curriculum, the university sponsored glee clubs, choruses, and instrumental ensembles as extracurricular activities. Alumni helped to organize similar groups off campus.

Almost every community of significant size had its own baseball team by the 1880s. Major businesses often supported their own teams as well. Charles A. Klinkner—printer, rubber stamp merchant, and "mayor" of the real estate development of Klinknerville—assembled the local nine for a photograph around 1886. Courtesy, Oakland Museum, History Department

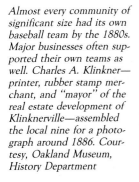

Duncan, the ethereal talent who would help shape the parameters of modern dance, lived in Oakland for the first 15 years of her life. In later years Florence Boynton, a lifelong friend, conducted a school of dance modeled on Duncan's philosophy in her Grecian-style home, the Temple of Wings.

South of the city that helped mold the free-spirited dancer another early 20th-century talent was creating dramatic change in an infant art form. The Essanay Film Manufacturing Company built a studio at Niles in 1913. Five of the 14 Essanay movies starring Charlie Chaplin, including what many consider his finest work, *The Tramp,* were filmed at Niles. *Rebecca of Sunnybrook Farm,* starring Mary Pickford, was filmed by Essanay at nearby Pleasanton in 1916.

THE ARCHITECTS

The University of California also played host to many of the key architectural designers of the late 19th and early 20th centuries. Bernard Maybeck, who taught descriptive geometry at the university in the 1890s, was a dominating figure in both the school's architecture and the School of Architecture. It was he who suggested the design competition underwritten by Phoebe Apperson Hearst, and his enthusiasm for that project as well as others aroused and inspired a group of East Bay architects including Julia Morgan.

Morgan was a much-admired and prolific architect whose projects ranged from modest homes to the rebuilding of the earthquake-ravaged Fairmont Hotel in San Francisco. Her San Francisco office produced designs for some 600 buildings, and many of these survive today. With Maybeck, she designed the Hearst Gymnasium for Women on the UC campus (which burned in 1922).

Although few of Maybeck's structures have survived, his legacy includes the work of his students, including Morgan, John Bakewell, and Arthur Brown, as well as that of the countless architects who found inspiration in his love of fantasy and his skill in combining old and new materials and structural forms drawn from the Gothic, Classical, Oriental, and vernacular traditions.

Completed in 1914, the Temple of Wings in the Berkeley Hills served as home and dance studio for the Charles Boynton family. The Berkeley fire of 1923 destroyed it, but the Boyntons rebuilt and continued the dance studio. Daughter Sulgwynn and husband Charles moved in permanently in 1946 and presented an annual Spring Dance Festival in the Isadora Duncan tradition until Sulgwynn's death in 1983. In this 1985 photograph, dancers participated in a "Thanksgiving" finale at a special Temple of Wings Spring Festival. Courtesy, Temple of Wings Collection, Margaretta K. Mitchell

The art of modern dance had its early beginnings in the family home of Isadora Duncan in the late 1880s and early 1890s. Duncan and friend Florence Treadwell Boynton as children taught neighborhood children to express their creativity through gesture and movement. Duncan left California in 1895 and became an international sensation, reviving ancient Greek dance forms and appearing in "scant" Grecian costumes which allowed freedom of movement. Courtesy, Margaretta K. Mitchell

Above: Bernard Maybeck, winner of the gold medal of the American Institute of Architects, is probably the Bay Area's best-known and best-loved architect. Courtesy, Oakland Museum, History Department

Right: Architect Julia Morgan was the first woman to graduate from the University of California in mechanical engineering and the first to graduate in architecture from the Ecole des Beaux Arts. She designed numerous residences in Berkeley, many of them garden-oriented and shingled or half-timbered. Most associate Morgan with her design of newspaper magnate William Randolph Hearst's "castle" in San Simeon. Courtesy, Chapel of the Chimes, Oakland

Other noted architects working in Alameda County in the early 20th century include Ernest Coxhead, Walter H. Ratcliff, Jr., George T. Plowman, John Hudson Thomas, Henry Higby Gutterson, Mark and John White, Randolph Monroe, and William Wilson Worster. Early Berkeley women architects include Katharine Underhill, Edna Deakin, Lilian Bridgman, and Leola Hall.

THE RELIGIOUS COMMUNITY

The connection between the artistic, spiritual, and educational movement locally has been long and close. Religious services preceded permanent edifices much as teaching generally began well before the school structures were erected. For most immigrants, their religious ties not only offered spiritual support, but also provided community and social services.

The Catholic heritage of Alameda County which began in 1797 with the establishment of Mission San Jose was continued in Oakland in 1858 when a priest was appointed to serve the young community. Other Catholic churches soon joined the St. Mary's Parish, serving the many ethnically diverse Catholic populations that have settled in the county. Roman Catholicism in the San Leandro area continues to reflect the large number of Portuguese citizens, who began arriving from the Azores in the 1860s. The entire community is welcome to attend the annual *Festa de Espirita Santa* (Feast of the Holy Ghost). A statue honoring the Portuguese immigrants, the work of the Portuguese sculptor Numidico Bessone, was erected at the northern boundary of Rancho San Leandro in 1964.

Followers of the Church of Jesus Christ of Latter-day Saints (Mormons) were next to establish a pattern of regular services in Alameda County. John Horner preached on Sunday mornings at the church/schoolhouse he built in Centerville in 1850; as the population increased, he made the building available to Presbyterians and Methodists on Sunday afternoons. In 1892 the Oakland First Ward, the oldest organized unit of the church in the state, was established as part of the California Mission. One of the landmarks of Alameda County is the modern Temple Hill complex dedicated by the Mormons in the 1960s and dominated by the Oakland Temple.

Protestant services began almost immediately with the arrival of the American settlers. The Reverend William Taylor, famous Methodist street preacher of San Francisco, offered a simple service to crews working in the redwoods in September 1849. Episcopalians who had been meeting in private homes invited the Reverend John Morgan from San Francisco to conduct services in a tent in 1853, but Morgan's boat became stuck on a sandbar. A Presbyterian minister in the audience, the Reverend Wadsworth, offered to preach, and within days the Presbyterians had bought the tent and organized the First Presbyterian Church of Oakland.

A circuit-riding Methodist minister, William Morrow, began holding services in 1853 at the Old Mission, Centerville, San Lorenzo, San Leandro, and Alameda. Methodists initiated services in a San Antonio schoolhouse in 1856 and organized the First Methodist Episcopal Church of Oakland in 1862.

Members of the First Baptist Church of Oakland, organized in 1854, were the first to worship in their own new building, a redwood structure at the corner of Fifth and Jefferson. Baptisms were performed in the Oakland estuary. In 1855 the Episcopalians formed St. John's Parish, the parent of several other congregations in Oakland and vicinity.

Future members of Oakland's First Congregational Church began holding services in borrowed churches in 1860 and moved into their own building in 1862. The first Unitarian Church, founded in 1875, traces its origins to a group who earlier withdrew from First Presbyterian of Oakland when the pastor was expelled for heresy. Zion Evangelical Lutheran Church, organized as a mission in 1880, became a formal congregation in 1882.

Berkeley's First Church of Christ, Scientist, is perhaps Bernard Maybeck's most brilliant achievement. The interior displays the architect's mastery of space, structure, color, and light. Because the congregation had limited funds, Maybeck's design called for the extensive use of natural wood, cast concrete, and industrial steel sash. Photo by Roy Flamm. Courtesy, Bancroft Library, University of California, Berkeley

Above: Pioneer congregations met first in private homes or schoolhouses, but soon established themselves in impressive houses of worship. This 1890 photograph taken at Clay, 13th, and 14th streets in Oakland shows (left to right) First Hebrew Congregation, Zion Evangelical Lutheran Church, and First Methodist Episcopal Church. The proximity of a synagogue to two Christian churches indicates the religious tolerance that typifies Alameda County. Courtesy, Oakland History Room, Oakland Public Library

Right: Constructed in Dublin in 1859, St. Raymond's was the first American-built Catholic church in Alameda County. Courtesy, Amador-Livermore Valley Historical Society

For those outside the mainstream of American life, the church provided a special sanctuary—a place to redefine the ancestral culture in relationship to the new environment. The earliest black congregation, First African Methodist Episcopal, grew out of a mission started by Isaac and Elizabeth Flood in 1858. The congregation bought Horace Carpentier's old schoolhouse in 1863, using it as both church and school until 1867 when a public school for black children was opened in Brooklyn. Two pioneer pastors, the Rever-

ends Jeremiah Sanderson and Thomas Myers Decatur Ward, led the congregation in spiritual, educational, cultural, and political programs.

Early Jewish families included dry-goods merchants Jacob Letter, Solomon Bell, Solomon Adler, and Samuel Herschberg (a former professor of classics at a Scottish university). In 1862 Herschberg formed a Hebrew Benevolent Society; this evolved into the First Hebrew Congregation of Oakland. A synagogue was dedicated in 1878, and three years later Meyer Solomon became the first rabbi. In California Jewish people became notable contributors to community, cultural, and educational institutions.

With the completion of the transcontinental railroad, large numbers of Chinese returned to settle in the East Bay. Unlike their Caucasian neighbors, these new residents were not quickly absorbed into the community. Since they were not allowed to become citizens, own land, or, except in rare instances, bring their families from China to live with them, these immigrants generally formed a bachelor society whose customs were abhorrent to their white neighbors. In addition to these "iniquities," the Chinese worshiped what were viewed as heathen gods.

After the earthquake of 1906, the presence in Oakland of several strong Protestant leaders influenced many Chinese to adopt the Christian faith. The first Chinese temple on Harrison Street was sold to a Jewish group and replaced with a smaller temple near the waterfront. In 1981, as a new wave of Asian immigration stimulated interest in Buddhism, Fut Quong Ji temple was built at Seventh and Oak streets under the direction of Mr. and Mrs. Peng Dot Keng and Bien Pak Kee.

Around 1900 a few Japanese moved to the East Bay and began holding monthly services under the direction of ministers from the Buddhist Church of San Francisco, the oldest Jodo Shinshu church in the continental U.S. The Oakland Buddhist Church was formed in 1901 and the first resident minister, the Reverend Mokuji Fuji, assigned in 1905.

In 1906 more than 14,000 Japanese settled in California, and Oakland was one of five major destinations. As their numbers increased, they were subjected to racist indignation similar to that visited upon the Chinese earlier. After meeting in residences for several years, the congregation built a Japanese-style temple at Sixth and Jackson. When they were forced to relocate during World War II, the evacuated members stored their personal belongings in the church. In the 1950s the temple was moved to its present location at Ninth and Jackson to make way for the Nimitz Freeway.

Eastern Orthodoxy, with its ancient liturgy and iconography, also enriches the spiritual heritage of Alameda County. In 1865 an exiled Ukrainian priest, Father Agapius Honcharenko, settled in the Hayward area, where he conducted services for many years. He published a bilingual newspaper, the *Alaska Herald-Svoboda,* and translated the United States Constitution for the Russian-speaking people of Alaska. Oakland's Greek Orthodox Church of the Assumption, while not organized until 1917, is the oldest in the East Bay and the second oldest in California.

In the 1960s a unique theological institution evolved out of Alameda County's position at the crossroads of many cultures. The Graduate Theological Union began as a consortium of four Protestant seminaries: Presbyterian, Baptist, Lutheran, and Episcopalian. They were soon joined by the Interdenominational Pacific School of Religion as well as by Dominican, Jesuit, Franciscan, and Unitarian faculties. Subsequently a Center for Judaic Studies, a Japanese Buddhist Study Center, and centers for Urban Black Studies, Women and Religion, Ethics and Social Policy, and Theology and the Natural Sciences were added. While the primary purpose remains the "providing of instruction on the graduate theological level," the GTU also serves as a place for both learning and appreciating the diversity that has long been a part of the West.

The Oakland Temple of the Church of Jesus Christ of Latter-day Saints dominates the Oakland hills skyline. Dedicated on November 17, 1964, the structure of reinforced concrete with four-inch Sierra marble facing rises 170 feet at the finial of the center spire. The center courtyard contains a reflecting pool fed by a waterfall down the temple's stylobate. Photo by David Lewis Wright. Courtesy, Clio: Public History Consultants by permission of the Oakland Temple, Church of Jesus Christ of Latter-day Saints

The Alameda County Tourist Association promoted Neptune Beach on the shores of the city of Alameda as a family playground and recreation area. This photo dates circa 1920. The facilities began to decline in the Depression and closed in 1939. Courtesy, California Section, California State Library,

CHAPTER 5

ON THE MOVE

The decades following the 1906 earthquake brought not only political changes to Alameda County but also developments in planning, industrialization, modernization, and the creation of numerous institutions. The once village-like atmosphere of the East Bay was to be transformed into the metro-complex familiar to us in the 20th century.

FIGHTING THE OCTOPUS

The Octopus by Frank Norris symbolized and aided the reform movement that followed its printing. Its social commentary and attack on the railroad's power would be manifest in Progressive Era politics. Pent-up public outrage with the political maneuvering of the monopoly finally produced results in 1907, when liberals who wanted to "free the Republican party from the shackles of the corporations" (meaning the Southern Pacific) formed the Lincoln-Roosevelt League.

A statewide meeting held in Oakland produced a "Platform of Principles" designed to end "boss rule," reform state politics, and campaign for the establishment of a direct primary in California. The league scored a major victory in 1909 with the adoption of a comprehensive primary law. Once again meeting in Oakland, the organization sought a viable gubernatorial candidate for the 1909 election. Oakland Mayor Frank K. Mott was considered, but Hiram Johnson was the final choice. Johnson carried the first Republican state primary because under the new system the Southern Pacific was unable to control the votes.

The first women's suffrage parade in California had occurred during the 1908 state Republican convention, held in Oakland. The 300 marchers were led by Lillian Coffin. By advocating women's suffrage the Republicans were seen as more liberal than the Democrats for the first time since the 1860s.

Johnson became governor in 1911 as the Republicans swept every state office. During Johnson's administration the initiative, referendum, and recall were instituted; the State Railroad Commission was authorized to control railroad rates; and nonpartisan election of judges, direct primary elections, and women's suffrage went into effect.

At the national level, a Progressive Party formed out of the liberal Republican wing, and in 1913 the Progressives in California, including Johnson, withdrew from the Republican Party. In 1914 Hiram Johnson was reelected.

Conservative Republicans opposed the far-reaching nature of Johnson's sweeping reforms. Led by Joseph R. Knowland's *Oakland Tribune,* along with the *Los Angeles Times* and the *San Francisco Chronicle,* the press continually lambasted the administration. However Johnson not only successfully completed his second term, but served as a U.S. senator from 1922 to 1940.

During this decade the county reflected the skillful leadership of Frank K. Mott, mayor of Oakland from 1905 to 1915.

Of all his achievements, it was Mott's handling of the waterfront properties that earned him his reputation as a far-sighted reformer. A 1907 court case, *Western Pacific vs. Southern Pacific,* brought the matter to a head. First, the U.S. Circuit Court held that the Southern Pacific could prevent the Western Pacific (not the Western Pacific Railroad previously absorbed by the Central Pacific) from building a track and wharf along the estuary. The U.S. Court of Appeals reexamined the issues and came up with a significant finding. In 1897 the state supreme court had rendered the crucial decision that, while the compromise of 1868 had validated Carpentier's claim to the land, the precise boundary of that land could be defined as the low-tide line of 1852. Furthermore, the court continued, because of dredging and filling, that line was by then well inland. (Curiously, earlier city authorities seem to have missed the significance of that ruling.) The court of appeals affirmed that the city indeed had the right to control all docks and other improvements to the tidelands as stated in the 1897 case. Following this major defeat, the Southern Pacific joined forces with the Western Pacific and proposed a bill to create a harbor commission (easily controlled by the railroad through its influence on the legislature) that would "relieve the city of all the bother of managing the harbor."

With the help of the *Oakland Enquirer,* Mott and others organized the Harbor League, which persuaded the legislature to kill the bill. Foreseeing an appeal to the Supreme Court,

which could have tied up the waterfront indefinitely, Mott met with a vice-president of the railroad and succeeded in negotiating a compromise that ended nearly 60 years of controversy. In return for a 50-year lease on the property it occupied, the Southern Pacific relinquished all claims to the waterfront. The Southern Pacific was secure in its access for the foreseeable future; the Western Pacific gained its wharf access; and the City of Oakland was in possession of its bay frontage, a fact which became even more important with the opening of the Panama Canal. Frank Mott was reelected mayor of Oakland by an overwhelming margin.

THE PROGRESSIVE ERA AND THE CITY BEAUTIFUL

During this period the City of Oakland consulted two world-famous city planners: Charles Mulford Robinson in 1906 and Werner Hegemann in 1915. Both stressed the urgency of preserving the natural beauty of Oakland by planning for parks, scenic avenues, a civic center, and less congested housing. While their recommendations were not completely carried out, their influence is highly visible in Oakland even today. Mott's popularity ensured the passage of bond issues totaling about eight million dollars for civic improvements.

The dream of a park on the shores of Lake Merritt was realized as the 12th Street Dam was improved, the lake dredged, and the swampland reclaimed, with a saltwater auxiliary system of fire protection installed at the lake's edge. The shoreline was landscaped and a boat landing, boathouse, and pergola built. The Josiah Stanford mansion (now the Camron-Stanford House) was transformed into the Oakland Public Museum. Several park sites were acquired. Oakland reached approximately its present boundaries in 1909 by annexing the suburbs of Claremont, Fruitvale, Leona Heights, Melrose, Fitchberg, Elmhurst, and other unincorporated territory.

Mott's attitude toward city planning coupled with a positive outlook toward industrial development made Oakland attractive to individuals and businesses alike. Among the buildings for which Mott's administration is

Sailing on the bay was a popular recreation around the turn of the century. The bridge in the background may be one of those connecting Oakland and Alameda. Courtesy, Amador-Livermore Valley Historical Society

remembered are Oakland Technical High School, the Claremont and Oakland hotels, and the auditorium.

With the adoption of a new city charter, Mott reorganized the police and fire departments, inaugurated a civil service system, and led the move to new street lighting, with electric and telephone wires placed underground. Industrial growth was phenomenal. Manufacturing activities grew by 150 percent with virtually all types of industry locating in the area. There were 450 factories in Oakland alone, with another 200 attracted to Alameda, Berkeley, San Leandro, and other communities.

The first eucalyptus groves of the East Bay were planted as windbreaks in the 1860s, but around 1904 the idea spread that the hardwood itself was valuable. Frank Havens sowed a plantation along the ridgetop from Redwood Peak to north Berkeley, with a scenic drive (Skyline Boulevard) running the full 14-mile length of the grove. Upon finding that the timber itself was useless, he and his associate F.M. "Borax" Smith, through their Realty Syndicate, developed 104 residential tracts on this and other property in the county. Meanwhile Smith, having gained control of all the East Bay street railways, overextended his resources in an attempt to add to his real estate and utility holdings. In 1913 he was forced into bankruptcy.

Above: Oakland's city hall—the first in the nation designed as a skyscraper—is shown here circa 1950. The trendsetting design was adopted for other city halls, including Los Angeles'. The cornerstone was dedicated on October 13, 1911, by President William Howard Taft. Courtesy, Oakland History Room, Oakland Public Library

Left: This postcard portrays the classic Queen Anne architecture of the Piedmont Baths, an important social hub in turn-of-the-century Alameda County. Meeting rooms, tearooms, and parlors (left and center) overshadowed the indoor pool (flattopped wing to the right). Courtesy, Ray Raineri

Other cities in the county also experienced growth that, while not as explosive as Oakland's, was still nothing short of dramatic.

Berkeley had established a town charter in 1895. In 1909 that document was amended to a city charter that replaced the old ward system with trustees elected at large. The new town hall begun in 1908 was dedicated as the city hall in August 1909. By 1910 Berkeley had a population of 40,000, making it California's fifth-largest city. Berkeley emerged as a leader in democratic city government with its system of public commissioners and boards, and in 1915 became the third city in the United States to adopt zoning and land-use regulations and one of the earliest to adopt the city-manager form of government.

August Vollmer became Berkeley's first chief of police in 1905. During his long and distinguished career Vollmer developed methods of criminology such as the lie-detector test and fingerprint classification, reorganized the department with motorized vehicles and radio communication, and redefined the role of the police to include prevention of crime and juvenile delinquency. He established a police training school that stressed professional standards of both skill and conduct. Berkeley gained renown as the home of one of the first modern police departments.

Newark experienced an economic boom between 1907 and 1910 when the Dumbarton bridge was constructed by the Southern Pacific Railroad. Once the bridge was completed, Newark became one of the busiest freight junctions in California. While Newark's industries were mostly small firms, the community did have the largest stove plant in California. James Graham's foundry had developed an easy-draft metal stove. This "Wedgewood" stove became tremendously popular and a standard for the industry.

WORLD WAR I

Further industrialization came with World War I. Wartime orders created an insatiable demand for vessels, and Oakland's shipbuilding facilities operated day and night. A committee organized to secure reserve workers for the shipyards, eventually registering more than 200,000 prospects. One 12,000-ton ship was built in 107 days—a record for the area. Experimental concrete ships were manufactured during this time as an attempt to conserve precious wartime steel supplies. Due to the area's emphasis on shipbuilding, the U.S. navy found Alameda County an especially good source for recruits. One naval vessel docked at Oakland

speech abridgement when police broke up their organizers. The IWW advocated violence as a means of achieving its goals, so the state legislature in 1919 passed a law providing for the arrest of anyone who advocated violence with regard to corporate or political change.

Anita Whitney was one of those brought to trial under the new law. The daughter of a former state senator from Alameda County, she was well known for her volunteer work with Oakland's charities. She was also a delegate to the Communist Labor Party convention in Oakland which advocated support of the IWW as well as revolutionary unionism. Whitney was convicted on felony charges because of her association with a group which "advocated, aided, or abetted criminal syndicalism." In 1927 Governor Clement C. Young, who was from Berkeley, pardoned 60-year-old Whitney, stating that it was "absolutely unthinkable to condemn . . . to a felon's cell this lifelong friend of the unfortunate."

In the post-World War I period, labor organizations grew to the point where organizers boasted a combined San Francisco-Alameda County membership of 100,000 with more power and influence than anywhere else in the West.

Left: World War I and the years immediately after brought boom conditions to Bay Area shipyards. The Moore Shipbuilding Company of Oakland launched a then-record six ships on October 11, 1919. Shown in this photo are the tankers City of Reno and Salina. Courtesy, Amador-Livermore Valley Historical Society

Below: Dozens of local women gathered in San Leandro for a rally and parade to promote the sale of Liberty Bonds after America entered World War I. Such spectacles were virtually necessary to sell the bonds, which had a 30-year maturity at 3.5 percent interest. Courtesy, California Section, California State Library

just for recruitment purposes.

Alameda's Government Island was built in 1915 as dredges enlarging a channel through Brooklyn Basin dumped their mud and dirt at that spot.

In San Leandro, the Best Company (which later became Caterpillar Tractor) was soon producing war equipment. All appropriate county industry retooled to supply the war effort.

Organized labor attempted to make advances, but employer resistance to demands for better pay and working conditions led to strikes. When Oakland's waterfront was crippled as more than 10,000 longshoremen walked off their jobs in 1916, the Oakland Chamber of Commerce passed a resolution declaring an "open shop" for the city, and employers lobbied for an anti-picketing law.

Throughout this period the International Workers of the World (IWW) opposed not only unfair labor conditions but the war itself. Openly vocal at Oakland's docks in an attempt to gain members, the IWW claimed free-

THE POSTWAR YEARS

With the end of the war in 1918, celebrations abounded. One parade of returning troops in Oakland was greeted by 100,000 onlookers. President Woodrow Wilson visited Oakland personally in September 1919, steaming into the estuary and staying in the Oakland Hotel. Flowers from San Leandro, famous for its dahlias, bedecked the presidential suite. The Alameda County Floral Society held its first annual dahlia show at the end of 1919—a symbol of a return to peace.

Oakland's destiny in the postwar years was guided by John L. Davie, who served as mayor from 1915-1931. Those four consecutive terms, when added to his previous service from 1895-1897, encompassed a quarter of the city's history up to that time. During his tenure, the voters approved a $9-million bond issued for harbor improvements, including the dredging of Lake Merritt. The continued development of the lake became Davie's personal quest; the long-proposed boulevard and Necklace of Lights encircling the lake were at last achieved. He had an island built for breeding wildfowl and worked (unsuccessfully) for a museum and recreational complex along the shore. Davie favored extending the role of municipal government to provide transportation, utility, and recreational services for the people. He was instrumental in the purchase of 300

The worldwide influenza epidemic of 1918-1919 forced officials to turn the Oakland Auditorium into a makeshift hospital with the assistance of Red Cross volunteers. More than 1,000 people died in Oakland as a result of the contagion. Courtesy, Oakland History Room, Oakland Public Library

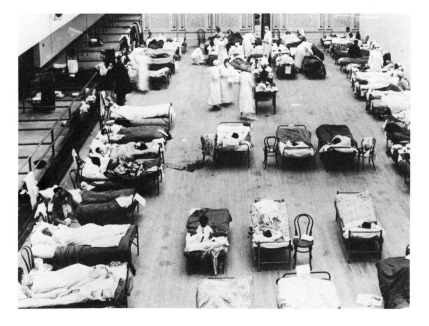

acres for Sequoia Park, which later became a part of the East Bay Regional Park District.

Among the most significant achievements of the Davie years was the establishment of the East Bay Municipal Utility District. As the burgeoning population required more and more water, a search for new supplies became imperative. The champion of this cause was none other than Oakland's George C. Pardee, former mayor of Oakland and governor of California, who felt that a separate water system would keep San Francisco from controlling the East Bay's lifeline. In 1921 the Municipal Utility District Act passed the California legislature. But only after the drought and Berkeley fire of 1923 did the voters of Richmond, El Cerrito, Oakland, Berkeley, Emeryville, Piedmont, Alameda, and San Leandro approve the formation of the East Bay Municipal Utility District (EBMUD).

Pardee was elected president of the new district. In 1924 a $39-million bond issue was passed for the construction of an aqueduct to the East Bay from the Mokelumne River. The source had been recommended by William Mulholland, chief engineer of the Los Angeles Aqueduct, and General George Goethals, builder of the Panama Canal, among others.

In 1929 the Pardee Dam on the Mokelumne and the almost 100-mile-long aqueduct were complete, and the East Bay had its precious water source. The dam was dedicated by Governor Clement C. Young. Pardee served as president of EBMUD until his death in 1941.

THE AUTOMOBILE AGE

During the 1920s Alameda County was one of the fastest-growing areas in the country. With the sustained increase in population came a new problem familiar today—automobile traffic. The Best gasoline motor carriage, built by Clarence and Daniel Best of San Leandro, made its first run in 1898. As the automobile increased in popularity, dust from roads became a serious problem. The county began oiling roads with crude petroleum in 1902. By 1916 use of the automobile was so widespread that Chevrolet opened an assembly plant in Oakland. Faegol, Ford, Durant, International Harvester, and Willys-Overland followed,

earning for the city the sobriquet "Detroit of the West."

Other industries that located or invested in Oakland were Western Electric, American Can, Sherwin-Williams, Westinghouse, Detroit Steel, Shell Oil, Albers Brothers Milling Company, and Western Waxed Paper, to name a few. Henry Kaiser chose Oakland as the headquarters for what would become his far-ranging industrial empire. In addition Oakland's skyline changed as the Tribune Tower was joined by such business establishments as Capwell's, I. Magnin, the Hotel Leamington, the Central Bank, and the Financial Center.

To alleviate the traffic problem and also spur industrial development, several major highway improvements were planned. In 1922 the Newark Chamber of Commerce, which had organized in 1909, campaigned for a highway bridge across the Dumbarton Narrows, closely paralleling the Southern Pacific's railroad line. On January 15, 1927, the Dumbarton highway bridge became the first to carry automobile traffic across San Francisco Bay. Soon another bridge connected Hayward with

San Mateo as cross-bay automobile access became more essential.

At the same time, a tunnel was planned from Oakland to Alameda under the Brooklyn Basin. In 1923 Alameda County passed a $4.5-million bond act for the Posey Tube project which, when finished, was the largest tunnel of its type in the world. Its completion allowed for major development of Oakland's port facilities, which had previously been hampered by bridges across the estuary.

Industrial development grew hand in hand with the new transportation systems. In Berkeley more than 100 new industrial plants were built in the 1920s. Manufacturing products as diverse as appliances and coconut oil, printing inks and airplanes, and chemical, bacteriological, and scientific instruments, Berkeley bustled economically. And this despite the holocaust that destroyed 584 buildings and damaged 100 more in September 1923. Between 1910 and 1930 Berkeley's population doubled. The city annexed the Claremont, Cragmont, Northbrae, and Thousand Oaks districts as its boundaries grew to modern proportions.

A ferry, a tugboat, and a rain-drenched crowd greet the arrival of the battleship Milwaukee *in this circa-1917 view of Oakland Municipal Dock No. 1. Courtesy, Oakland History Room, Oakland Public Library*

Above: The Durant Automobile Company opened its Oakland assembly plant in 1922. Oakland Mayor John L. Davie, who wanted Oakland to become the "Detroit of the West," drove the first car off the assembly line. (The driver in this picture is unknown.) Chevrolet, Willys, Faegol, Caterpillar, International Harvester, and Chrysler all manufactured vehicles in or around Oakland at different times. Courtesy, William F. Harrah Automobile Foundation

Right: The Faegol automobile, built by an Oakland-based manufacturer, was intended to be the American equivalent of the Rolls Royce. Price tags as high as $17,000 guaranteed a limited market. About 1,500 vehicles were produced in 1917-1918 before Faegol switched to the more lucrative production of trucks and buses until going out of business in 1932. Courtesy, William F. Harrah Automobile Foundation

Salt production, among the area's earliest industries, increased dramatically as large concerns bought out the pioneer firms. In 1919 August Schilling of Schilling Spice fame started the Arden Salt Company at Dumbarton Point, eventually purchasing bay land all the way to the Santa Clara County line. Morton Salt Company opened a processing and marketing plant in 1925. In 1927 the Leslie California Company acquired the Plummer Salt Works at Alvarado and bought more land bordering the bay. Leslie absorbed Arden in 1936, becoming the largest landholder in the Bay Area. The Newark salt concentration ponds were also utilized by such firms as Westvaco Chlorine Products and California Chemical Company, who extracted minerals from the waste seawater.

The Alameda Sugar Company, which took over the Standard Sugar Manufacturing Company in 1890, closed briefly during 1914, but was reactivated within the year to supply sugar to the armed forces. In 1925 Holly Sugar of Utah bought the plant, which it operated until moving to Tracy in 1969.

THE PORT OF OAKLAND COMES INTO ITS OWN

On January 20, 1927, the Oakland City Council voted to establish an independent Board of Port Commissioners to administer the waterfront properties. The action required a charter amendment which passed overwhelmingly despite the opposition of Mayor Davie. The new commission included attorney Roscoe Jones, pharmacist Robert Leet, department store magnate H.C. Capwell, and George Pardee. Construction and commerce along the waterfront boomed and the port prospered with some 15 shipbuilding facilities established in the area.

Air travel was also on the horizon. Amateur aviators had begun experimenting with hot air balloons, gliders, and dirigibles soon after the Wright brothers' successful flight in 1903. The first powered flight in Alameda County may have occurred on September 22, 1909, when Fong Joe Guey piloted his homemade biplane over the hills of Piedmont. Weldon Bagster Cooke made a powered flight

over Oakland on Columbus Day, 1911. William Beachey, a popular local stunt flier, was killed while performing at the Panama-Pacific Exposition in 1915.

In 1927 the city council authorized the purchase of nearly 700 acres of Bay Farm Island for an airport, to come under the jurisdiction of the Port Commissioners. In so doing, they outfoxed the San Francisco authorities, who had been eyeing the property for an airport of their own. By June a runway nearly a mile and a half in length had been constructed, the largest in the world at the time. Later that month Lieutenant Albert Hegenberger and Lieutenant Lester Maitland took off in a military bomber bound for Hawaii. Only a month earlier Charles Lindbergh had become the first to fly across the Atlantic Ocean, and the army hoped to duplicate that accomplishment in the Pacific. Hegenberger and Maitland were thrust into prominence after completing the first trans-Pacific crossing with a day-long flight. Upon their return to Oakland they were greeted by thousands of cheering residents.

The rush for fame and notoriety during this new era of aviation had its humorous as well as dramatic moments. In July 1927 Ernie Smith and Emery Bronte became the first civilians to pilot a plane to Hawaii. Taking off from

Above: On September 17, 1923, a terrible fire ravaged the city of Berkeley. By the time the flames were extinguished, 584 family residences, apartment houses, fraternities, sororities, and a firehouse were destroyed, and 100 more structures were damaged. Courtesy, Berkeley Historical Society

Facing page, inset: Best's Horseless Carriage was the first automobile built and seen in Alameda County. Assembled at the Best Manufacturing Company in 1898, it featured a seven-horsepower, vapor-electric, water-cooled gasoline engine with two opposed cylinders. Top speed was almost 20 miles per hour. Clarence Lee Best is at the wheel. Courtesy, San Leandro Community Library Center

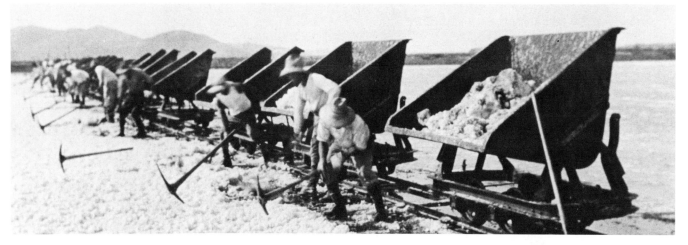

Oakland Municipal Airport, they crossed the Pacific and crashed in a tree on Molokai as their fuel ran out. Uninjured, they climbed down the tree amid startled onlookers who had never seen an airplane and issued those now immortal words, "Hi. We just flew in from California. Anybody got a cigarette?"

With these dazzling feats, Oakland's airport received national attention. When, in August 1927, James Dole, Hawaii's pineapple baron, offered a $25,000 prize in an Oakland-to-Hawaii race, the press converged on Bay Farm Island. Thousands watched as nine planes took off in hopes of capturing the prize. The danger of this new form of transportation became apparent when only two planes finished the race. Ten fliers perished in the attempt. Some were never recovered from their ocean graves.

Hazardous or not, Alamedans loved their new airport and its flying heros and heroines. Thousands again flocked to watch as Colonel Lindbergh landed his *Spirit of St. Louis* in 1927, and in 1931 as Amelia Earhart arrived completing the first transcontinental flight of an autogiro. In 1935 Earhart again landed in Oakland, completing the first solo flight from Hawaii to the U.S. mainland. And it was in Oakland that she began the fateful around-the-world journey that ended with her disappearance in the South Pacific.

Soon transcontinental passenger and airmail service became commonplace, with United and TWA having regular flights to and from Oakland. The airport was one of the six largest airmail centers in the United States, responsible for the distribution of all the Bay Area airmail.

Right: Jack London Square, is a six-block area centered around the foot of Broadway on the Oakland Estuary. Adjacent Jack London Village, shown here, adds a pleasant multilevel enclave of restaurants, shops, plazas, and an art gallery. Photo by John Elk III

Below: University of California students relax outside the South Hall, the first university building constructed by the state (in 1872) and the first UC structure to undergo earthquake safety improvements under the 1986 state bond issue. Photo by John Elk III

*Above: Livermore's Hindu
Community and Cultural
Center honors two major
and eight minor deities.
The temple of Shiva, left
rear, is built in the rectil-
inear Kalinga style of
northern India, while that
of Lord Vishnu, right rear,
shows the ornate Chola
style of the south. The center is open to the public.
Courtesy, Hindu Com-
munity and Cultural
Center, Inc.*

Left: Superior facilities at the Port of Oakland's outer harbor, shown here, accommodate direct traffic to and from both European and Far Eastern ports. By increasing exports 40 percent from 1976 to 1986, Oakland became the first major American port to receive the Department of Commerce's coveted E-Star Award. Photo by John Elk III

Facing page: The Pleasanton-Dublin area, in foreground, is among the fastest growing business centers in Northern California. Interstate Highway 580 (named for former Senator Arthur H. Breed, Jr., between Dublin and Castro Valley) connects the interior valleys with the San Francisco-Oakland Bay Bridge and north-south Interstate Highway 880 (named for Fleet Admiral Chester A. Nimitz). Courtesy, Pacific Aerial Surveys

Strong, summer winds and the possibility of land use compatible with dry farming and grazing attracted the first wind-energy producers to the Altamont Pass area in 1981. Electricity produced by the 7,600 wind turbines, is fed into the Pacific Gas and Electric Company system. In 1987 the windmills produced 874,723,378 million kilowatt hours of power, equivalent to the output of nearly 1.5 million barrels of oil, and sufficient to supply 145,787 California families for one year. Photo by Jordan Coonrad

Above: Once heavily industrial, Emeryville now hosts bio-tech and computer companies, office complexes, condominiums, restaurants, shops, and a harbor for pleasure craft. Almost 10 percent of the population are working visual artists. This is believed to be the highest number of artists per captia of any urban area in the country. Photo by Mark E. Gibson

Right: Ten miles south of Livermore, Del Valle Regional Park features a five-mile-long lake popular with boaters, windsurfers, anglers, and those seeking relief from the heat. Courtesy, East Bay Regional Park District

Del Valle Reservoir, just south of Livermore, forms the focus for a 4,000-acre regional park with facilities for picnicking and a wide variety of recreational activities. Del Valle is the eastern gateway to the Ohlone Wilderness Trail. Courtesy, Pacific Aerial Surveys

Left: Famous aviatrix Amelia Earhart based her long-distance flights to destinations across the Pacific Ocean at Oakland Airport. In 1935 Earhart flew non-stop from Honolulu to Oakland, a distance greater than Charles Lindbergh's transatlantic flight of 1927. Courtesy, Oakland Museum, History Department

Facing page: These hikers approaching the summit of Mission Peak will soon be rewarded with a view of Mt. Hamilton, the Santa Cruz Mountains, Mt. Tamalpais, Mt. Diablo, and the Central Valley. The 2,596-acre Mission Peak Regional Preserve lies near Fremont. Courtesy, East Bay Regional Park District

Left: In the early days of commercial flight, Oakland promoted itself as the East Bay's leading aviation facility. This photo is from a 1929 advertisement postcard. Courtesy, California Section, California State Library

Bay Bridge cables finally linked San Francisco to Oakland in 1935. The following year saw the span completed and opened to automobile traffic. From the Moulin Collection. Courtesy, Oakland Museum, History Department

CHAPTER 6

GROWING PAINS

The Alameda County waterfront was booming as the 1920s drew to a close. The bay was alive with ferries, with sailings every few minutes during peak hours from the Southern Pacific Mole and Key System Pier. More than 47,000 passengers rode the ferries in 1930; of these crossings, 27,000 were between Oakland and San Francisco. The traffic was not entirely local. Except for those who came from Southern California, all tourists visiting San Francisco arrived by boat. The Southern Pacific added three automobile ferries to its fleet in 1929.

The port too was prospering. The Grove Street and Outer Harbor terminals had been completed; the Ninth Avenue Double Pier was under way; and at the Municipal Airport a new passenger terminal adjoined the nation's first airport inn.

CHALLENGE AND CHANGE IN THE THIRTIES

The need for a bridge between Oakland and San Francisco had been discussed since World War I, but the engineering problems, the expense, and the opposition of the War Department were thought to present insurmountable obstacles. However, with the election in November 1928 of a Californian, Herbert Hoover, to the presidency, state and local officials found an ally.

Hoover and Governor Clement C. Young (from Berkeley) appointed a commission to propose a bridge that would reconcile the needs of national defense, navigation, and cross-bay traffic. Mark L. Requa, an engineer from Piedmont, was chairman; the San Francisco publisher George T. Cameron, vice-chairman; and C.H. Purcell, the state highway engineer, secretary. Senator Arthur H. Breed, Sr., represented Alameda County and Professor Charles D. Marx the University of California. The War Department was represented by Brigadier General G.B. Pillsbury, Lieutenant Colonel B.L. Dailey, Rear Admiral W.H. Standley, and Rear Admiral Luther E. Gregory, USN Ret. The commission convened on October 7, 1929, and 10 months later recommended a high-level bridge from Rincon Hill to Yerba Buena Island and thence along the route of the Key System Pier to the east shore.

The California Toll Bridge Authority was created, and the venture begun. When financing the project bogged down, Joseph R. Knowland secured a loan from the Reconstruction Finance Corporation. It was expected that the project would create 6,000 new jobs in the Bay Area and another 5,000 elsewhere in the country. On November 12, 1936, the San Francisco-Oakland Bay Bridge opened amid much fanfare.

When the Depression struck the country in 1929, Alameda County suffered economic setbacks as well as the human misery accompanying such financial collapse. One of the county's largest employers, the Key System, went into receivership. Alameda County's Welfare Council increased its caseload more than 800 percent between 1929 and 1932.

Union activity on the waterfront flared up after the passage of the National Industrial Recovery Act which guaranteed workers the right to organize and choose their own representatives. San Francisco workers organized a local of the International Longshoremen's Union, demanding better wages and working conditions, union-controlled hiring halls, and an agreement requiring all Pacific Coast ports to support one another's strikes.

Violence erupted in 1934. A battle between 5,000-6,000 pickets and 1,000 San Francisco police resulted in 60 injuries and two deaths. Labor responded by calling a general strike, which lasted from July 16 through July 19. More than 125 Bay Area unions, including 70 from Oakland, participated. When the public withdrew its support, the matter was submitted to arbitration and the unions got their hiring halls.

The working conditions of black railroaders were improved by the efforts of Cottrell Laurence Dellums, who came to Oakland in the early 1920s. In 1937, as vice-president of the International Brotherhood of Sleeping Car Porters, he secured recognition of the brotherhood by the Pullman Company, whose anti-union tactics were infamous. Dellums also helped in opening shipyards, as well as all war industry, to black workers. In 1968 he became president of the union, a position he held for 10 years.

As the Depression took its toll, the cost of medical care became prohibitive for many. In 1936 the Alameda County Medical Association and seven hospitals (Peralta, Providence, Merritt, Alameda, East Oakland, Alta Bates, and Berkeley General) contributed funds to incorporate the state's first hospital insurance plan for the general public. Blue Cross of

Northern California was headquartered in Oakland until 1982, when it merged with its Southern California counterpart.

PRESERVING THE WILDERNESS

Alameda County residents have long supported conservation efforts.

In the 1920s Duncan McDuffie, chairman of the Save-the-Redwoods League's State Parks Committee, assisted with galvanizing a state parks movement. In 1925 Arthur H. Breed, Sr., who represented Alameda County

May, representing the UC Bureau of Public Administration, and Hollis Thompson, Berkeley city manager, community conservation and recreation groups formed an association to petition the EBMUD to set aside and maintain 10,000 acres as parklands. When the district refused, Oakland's Kahn Foundation financed a comprehensive survey of the recreational needs of the East Bay communities. Armed with this Olmsted-Hall survey, the mayors of Alameda and Contra Costa County cities organized a board under the chairmanship of Elbert M. Vail of Oakland to lobby the legislature for the creation of the special district that

Bottom: This Depression-era photo shows students of Berkeley's Columbus School working their own garden plot in 1932. The Western Gardeners Corporation provided assistance and materials. Courtesy, Berkeley Historical Society

Left: Not all suffered during the Depression. Wine-making families of the Livermore Valley took advantage of the repeal of Prohibition in 1933. Family and workers posed at the Concannon winery in 1934 after planting a new vineyard. Courtesy, Amador-Livermore Valley Historical Society

in the state senate between 1913 and 1935, introduced legislation creating the State Park System. Governor Friend Richardson, from Berkeley, vetoed the bill. Undaunted, McDuffie organized support for the nomination of Lieutenant Governor Clement C. Young to replace Richardson in the next election. With Young's election as governor, Breed again introduced the enabling legislation, and Governor Young signed it into law in 1927. McDuffie and Breed next lent their support to the creation of the East Bay Regional Park District (EBRPD).

Every city planner ever consulted by the City of Oakland had stressed the importance of setting aside scenic hillsides, creeks, and canyons as parklands, and some progress had been made. However when the East Bay Municipal Utility District declared such lands to be surplus in 1928, community leaders were galvanized into action.

Led by Robert Sibley, executive director of the UC Alumnae Association, Samuel C.

Alameda, the estuary, Oakland, and the curving Key System pier are shown here in one of the last photographs made before work on the San Francisco-Oakland Bay Bridge became visible above the water. Although there was concern that bridging the bay would somehow deface its natural beauty, the oddly incomplete look of this 1933 photograph shows how much those immense human creations have come to seem a part of the natural environment. Courtesy, Pacific Aerial Surveys

This 1936 photograph shows the Broadway Low-Level Tunnel under construction, viewed from Contra Costa. Highway 24 follows this route today. The Contra Costa Tunnel, built in 1903 and replaced by the new tunnel, is seen in the upper portion of the photo. Alameda County's Assemblyman (and later Senator) Arthur H. Breed, Jr., secured a legislative appropriation for the Broadway Low-Level Tunnel, which was opened in 1937. After the completion of a third bore in 1964 the tunnels were rededicated in the name of Thomas E. Caldecott, president of the Board of Directors of Joint Highway District #13. Courtesy, Contra Costa County Historical Society

would be required. Every type of community group participated in an effort to get out the vote. Major Charles L. Tilden, Samuel May, Harlan Frederick, and Fred Reed were influential among the organizers. AB1114, drafted by Assemblyman and former Oakland Mayor Frank K. Mott, was passed in 1933.

Although Contra Costa County withdrew from the effort, Alameda, Albany, Berkeley, Emeryville, Oakland, Piedmont, and San Leandro voted to support the East Bay Regional Park District with a five-cent tax increase. Since the district was without funds at first, Tilden advanced the money for the purchase of the first 60 acres. General Manager Elbert Vail, serving at first without pay, arranged for contributions of labor ultimately totaling three million dollars from the Civilian Conservation Corps, the Works Progress Administration, and the Public Works Administration. The Utah Construction and Mining Company donated materials left over from the construction of the nearby Broadway Low-Level Tunnel. Thus, while the Depression took its toll, that period also witnessed changes that preserved forever the scenic wilderness areas of Alameda County.

WORLD WAR II

World War II had a profound effect on the Bay Area and brought about changes in society that were at least equal to the effects of the Gold Rush. The economic stimulus encouraged diversification of industry, while creating massive social disruptions.

The Japanese bombing of Pearl Harbor on December 7, 1941, outraged and terrified the people of the Pacific Coast. Amid feelings of fear and hysteria, Civil Defense spotters scanned the skies, all large gatherings were prohibited, and blackouts were instituted, including the "Necklace of Lights" around Lake Merritt. An order signed by President Franklin D. Roosevelt required all persons of Japanese ancestry to appear on April 30, 1942, for evacuation to remote camps and barracks, taking only minimal personal effects.

East Bay industries worked around the clock manufacturing materials for the war effort. Private shipyards such as Alameda's Bethlehem Steel Shipbuilding Division and Oakland's Moore Dry Dock Company became essentially military producers. Moore alone employed nearly 38,000 workers, and the combined Bay Area shipyard payroll reached nearly $40 million. Oakland's Henry Kaiser established seven shipyards which, by the end of the war, had produced nearly one-third of the entire U.S. merchant fleet.

Processing and packing food for the armed forces was second only to shipbuilding in economic importance; other war-related occupations included the production of blood plasma, drugs, life rafts, rope ladders, printed forms, steel drums, truck bodies, bomb fins, and special paints. Thousands found work supplying the needs of the growing working class.

Alameda Naval Air Station was completed in 1940, and the Oakland Naval Supply Depot was commissioned on December 8, 1941. The Pacific Naval Air Bases Command, the Army Quartermaster Corps, the War Shipping Administration, and the Coast Guard were soon firmly established in the county. In Emeryville the Ordinance Automotive Shop would service more than 200,000 vehicles by war's end and employ women as convoy drivers. All commercial flights were diverted to San Francisco as Oakland became the departure

Deputy County Clerk Helen Power administered the oath for Assemblyman Arthur Breed, Jr., as he filed his nomination papers at the county courthouse June 12, 1942. Representing Alameda County, Breed served four years in the state assembly and 20 years in the state senate. He sponsored legislation funding the Broadway Low-Level Tunnel and creating the Alameda-Contra Costa Transit and Bay Area Rapid Transit districts, and also worked on behalf of the University of California, the Port of Oakland, and the East Bay Municipal Utility and East Bay Regional Park districts. Courtesy, Oakland Tribune

point for all Pacific-bound military aircraft. Oakland's Municipal Airport would be slow to recover from the loss of commercial business diverted during that period.

Alameda County also played a major role in critical theoretical research which eventually held the key to ending the war itself. By the late 1930s the University of California at Berkeley had become one of the world's outstanding institutions of higher education. With the discovery of nuclear fission in 1938, theoretical physicists around the world worked on its practical application for military use. Dr. Robert Oppenheimer, a physicist already working in the field, was asked to direct a small group of scientists at Berkeley in planning the production of an atomic bomb.

A 1942 meeting of that group at Le Conte Hall remains one of modern history's most significant conferences. Oppenheimer, along with Ernest O. Lawrence, after whom UCB's Hall of Science in Berkeley and Radiation Laboratory in Livermore are named, and Edward Teller, the "father of the hydrogen bomb," were also active participants in finding the key to fission's "practical" uses. As a result of his work at Berkeley, Oppenheimer was appointed director of the Los Alamos facility that ultimately detonated the first atomic bomb, hastening the end of the war with the bombing of Hiroshima.

All of these programs and installations attracted untold thousands of job seekers. The East Bay's population increased by half a million between 1941 and 1945. Berkeley grew by about 30 percent, and Oakland from 302,163 to 400,936. The sudden increase strained the city and county services almost to the breaking point. Because of the housing shortage, many had to commute from other areas to their defense jobs, which made the transportation problem more acute than in any other part of the United States.

Even more disruptive than the overcrowding was the composition of the new work force. The employment of women, migrants from rural areas, and Asians required some adjustments, as did the massive influx of blacks. Before the war, blacks had made up only 2.4 percent of California's population. Now, attracted by the opportunity for a better life, they flocked to the Bay Area by the thousands. In Oakland their numbers grew from 8,462 in 1940 to 47,562 in 1950—an increase from 3 percent to 12.4 percent of the city's population in 10 years. Because of their disinclination to meld with Oakland's established black middle class, they were especially resented. They were segregated into "auxiliary" unions and given the less desirable graveyard shifts.

Sexual and racial prejudices occasionally resulted in violent incidents in the war plants, in the housing projects, and on the streets.

Left: A Berkeley couple of Japanese ancestry awaited transport to a federal relocation center in May 1942. Years later some of the interned recalled that they left their homes dressed in their best clothes in a quiet display of pride and dignity. Courtesy, Berkeley Historical Society

AFTER THE WAR

Planning for the postwar conversion to a peacetime economy began even as the war raged on. Meeting in Oakland in August 1944, state legislators, local officials, industrialists, and business leaders found that three-fourths of the wartime newcomers planned to stay. Cooperative efforts by the private and public sectors would be required to provide the necessary jobs and facilities.

Education was high on the list of priorities. The community college system was expanded to make vocational and academic training readily available in every part of the county. The Peralta district serves the north county with Alameda, Feather River, Vista, Laney, and Merritt colleges and the Oakland Skills Center; the Chabot district maintains campuses in Livermore and Hayward; and Ohlone College serves the Fremont/Newark area. The State College for Alameda County, established in 1959, was granted university status as California State University, Hayward, in 1972.

As the population of Alameda County continued to increase, highway traffic was at congestion levels never before seen. At the same time, the increased use of the automobile and the bridges had eliminated the historic transportation systems. The Southern Pacific terminated its East Bay interurban and trans-

bay operations in 1941. The steam locomotive made its last local run in 1954. In community after community, public transportation systems dwindled from their once-effective proportions.

The East Bay's first freeway, the Eastshore, was opened in 1949 and later named for Admiral Chester Nimitz. Soon the county was crisscrossed with numerous multilane highways and overpasses. Eastern Alameda County was connected by a freeway from the bay through Castro Valley, Dublin, Pleasanton, and Livermore, which fostered increased urbanization of the Livermore Valley. The impact of Interstate Highways 580 and 680 even moved the town of Pleasanton to vote against further development.

Above: Southern Alameda County canneries have been among California's largest processors of tomatoes since the 1890s. Food processing was especially important during the World War II era, when this photograph was taken. Courtesy, Hayward Area Historical Society

Above: National defense requirements led to the creation of small military sites in outlying areas of Alameda County in the 1940s. Personnel and their families had to tolerate particular hardships of living near military craft as did those quartered at the Livermore Naval Air Station in 1953. Photo by J. Oxley Moore. Courtesy, National Archives and Records Administration, San Bruno, California

Above, right: The city of Alameda served as home to two maritime institutions: the Alameda Naval Air Station (background), still in operation, and the U.S. Maritime Training Station (foreground), which served until the early 1960s. Photo by R.L. Copeland. Courtesy, National Archives and Records Administration, San Bruno, California

Right: In 1946 pioneer atomic scientists inspected the 184-inch pole faces of the 4,000-ton magnetic cyclotron at the Lawrence Berkeley Laboratory. From left to right are Dr. Donald Cooksey, assistant director, Radiation Laboratory; Dr. Ernest O. Lawrence, director of the laboratory; Professor Robert Oppenheimer; and William Brobeck, assistant engineer in charge of the cyclotron. Courtesy, Oakland Tribune

Southwest Alameda County grew to such an extent that traditional communities regrouped to form more effective political units. Newark incorporated as a city in 1955 to forestall inclusion in the new city of Fremont, formed from the districts of Mission San Jose, Niles, Centerville, Irvington, and Warm Springs the following year. The towns of Alvarado and Decoto incorporated in 1959 as Union City, electing Tom Kitayama as the first Japanese-American mayor in California.

In the central county, Dublin incorporated, and Hayward annexed Mt. Eden, extending its boundaries southward to Whipple Road. San Lorenzo and Castro Valley elected to continue as unincorporated communities.

In 1953 an 11-week transit strike occurred against the Key System. The shut-down crippled the company. In October 1959 voters passed a $16.5-million bond issue to purchase the system and establish the Alameda-Contra Costa Transit District (AC). Had AC not been formed, the area's highway system would have been incapable of handling the increased load.

In 1957 the Utah Construction Company completed the largest bay-fill operation of its day when 335 acres of tideland was reclaimed and added to the Alameda shoreline. This new land accommodated housing for more than 12,000 additional people. The Berkeley Hills also became a sought-after housing location.

With the destruction of open space and the increased presence of the automobile, pollution became a serious problem. The bay had become critically contaminated with World War II industrial producers' wastes. New sewage-treatment plants were constructed and a regional water-pollution control board formed. In 1955 a similar district was authorized to counter problems with air pollution.

THE WARREN YEARS

Although voter registration became preponderantly Democratic in the 1950s, Republican influence continued to be strong, due in part to superior party organization, in part to the custom of cross-filing in elections, and perhaps most of all to the leadership talents of Earl Warren.

Above: Soldiers, sailors, and marines joined local young women in a formal celebration at the end of World War II in a Hayward Victory Dance on August 24, 1945. Courtesy, Hayward Area Historical Society

Left: Confetti and streamers rained on celebrants at B and Main in downtown Hayward on August 14, 1945, as the announcement of V-J Day meant the end of World War II. Courtesy, Hayward Area Historical Society

Modern automobile traffic did not deter a traditional cattle drive in 1940 Livermore. The herd crossed the railroad tracks at First Street. Courtesy, Amador-Livermore Valley Historical Society

As district attorney of Alameda County in the 1930s, Warren became known as a formidable enemy of organized crime. With the backing of the *Oakland Tribune* he was elected attorney general in 1942 and then governor of California, serving an unprecedented three terms from 1943-1953. Although a Republican, Warren gave the impression of being nonpartisan. His highly successful administration is known for cutting taxes, building highways, mediation of labor disputes, developing a water-use and conservation program, and improving medical care, unemployment insurance, old-age pensions, and welfare payments to families with dependent children. As governor, he pushed—unsuccessfully—for fair employment and nondiscrimination statutes binding on unions and employers alike.

Later, as chief justice, Warren liberalized the U.S. Supreme Court. He wrote and delivered the landmark desegregation decision of 1954 which helped inaugurate the civil rights revolution still under way. He also supported the one-man-one-vote reapportionment amendment.

In the 1958 election—perhaps the political debacle of the era—Alameda County lost the Senatorial seat held since 1945 by William Fife Knowland, the son of publisher and former Congressman Joseph Knowland. The younger Knowland had gained national prominence as California's senior senator, serving as majority leader and later minority leader of that august body. He appeared assured of re-election.

Warren's successor as governor, Goodwin J. Knight, was also expected to serve another term. Conservative Republicans, however, having decided that Knight was too liberal, backed Knowland in a bid for the governorship, which they saw as a stepping-stone to the presidency. Knight was forced to run for Knowland's vacated seat in the Senate. Campaigning on opposite sides of the Right-to-Work issue, both were defeated.

Democratic candidates swept every state office except that of secretary of state. Oakland's black community gained political recognition with the appointment of Lionel Wilson to the municipal court in 1960 and Joshua Rose to the city council in 1964.

THE TURBULENT SIXTIES

With the events of the 1960s Alameda County was thrust into the world limelight. That turbulent, stimulating period was perhaps a culmination of the pressures of previous decades. Rapid cultural changes, heightened urbanization, and the intellectual stimulus fostered by the University of California all contributed to a decade that will be forever discussed and analyzed by historians.

Political activism at UCB actually began in the 1950s with worries over communist infiltration in the country. The university implemented and enforced a loyalty oath which, between 1950 and 1956, caused the resignation of many of the teaching staff. But it was in the vocalization of concern about the national issues of the 1960s—the civil rights movement and the Vietnam War—that the East Bay mirrored, or perhaps magnified, the country's social unrest.

In the fall of 1964, student activists gathered at Sather Gate to recruit supporters. The administration enforced an old rule against such solicitation on university property, triggering a massive movement that came to be known as the Free Speech Movement—the right of students to participate in politics on campus.

Led by the charismatic Mario Savio, the movement gained supporters among students, nonstudents, and faculty. Issues were broadened to include not only student approval of

Left: By the mid-1950s a growing population had transformed much of the southwestern county from farms to suburban communities. Decoto (foreground) became a part of Union City, while Niles (right center) was one of five districts combining to form the city of Fremont. Courtesy, Pacific Aerial Surveys

Below: Earl Warren served as Alameda County district attorney from 1925 to 1939, state attorney general from 1939 to 1943, and governor of California from 1943 until 1953, when President Eisenhower appointed him California's first chief justice of the United States. Significant decisions rendered by the Supreme Court during Warren's tenure profoundly affected the course of American history by effecting the desegregation of public schools, safeguarding the rights of the accused, and altering the traditional method of legislative apportionment to increase the representation of metropolitan areas. Courtesy, San Francisco Chronicle

university policies regarding teaching, research, course content, and admissions, but such unacademic issues as legalizing pot, ending the draft, eliminating ROTC, banning military recruiting, and closing the university's Lawrence Livermore Laboratory. Rebuffed, they used the tactics learned in off-campus protest movements—climaxing with a sit-in in Sproul Hall, the nominal nerve center of the university. State police were called out to clear the building, and more than 700 persons, not all of them students, were arrested. Massive sit-ins and forms of open protest occurred, amplified by an antiwar mood in the area. In 1965 and 1967 protesters marched from Berkeley to Oakland in a growing series of demonstrations that by then were sweeping the nation.

The protests became bloody in 1967 when the Black Panther Party, which had been organized in Oakland by two Merritt College students, Huey Newton and Bobby Seale, had a shootout with police. One police officer died and Newton was injured. Newton was convicted of voluntary manslaughter. In another confrontation, one Black Panther died, while Panther leader Eldridge Cleaver and four police were wounded.

Equally infamous were the People's Park demonstrations in 1969. When UCB decided to convert a grassy area of open space into a parking lot, demonstrations erupted. The resulting violence left one person dead as Alameda County sheriff's deputies defended themselves.

With the end of the Vietnam War, protest subsided. Much had been accomplished during those trying years, although the human price paid was high.

Limits of all kinds were tested and defied. Leaders and lawmakers, struggling to effect the transition from wartime to peacetime economy, found their work complicated by strident demands from groups whose priorities and values were contradictory to social norms and also often with one another. Scientific, medical, technological, and economic barriers were broken, often with unforeseen consequences.

The county had survived its share of labor strife as well as social and political experimentation and protest. Small towns like San Leandro and Hayward were transformed into industrial entities of their own with dramatic rates of growth in the 1950s and 1960s. In the mid-1960s, Alameda became the first Northern California county with a population in excess of one million individuals.

Left: In 1969 UC Berkeley students assembled near University Hill in protest while University of California regents met to discuss policy matters. National Guard patrols were called in to preserve order. Courtesy, Oakland Tribune

Below: By 1973 the Black Panthers, while still given to occasional violence among themselves, were sponsoring such programs as food distribution to Oakland's poor (shown), school breakfasts, and sickle cell anemia tests. But even while the Panthers turned to constructive participation in society, violence continued. On November 7, 1973, the Symbionese Liberation Army assassinated Oakland Schools Superintendent Marcus Foster, a black educator nationally famous for promoting racial harmony. The following February the SLA kidnapped Patricia Hearst. Courtesy, Oakland Tribune

The alluvial plain west of the mountains is now almost completely urbanized, and modern highways make the interior valleys quickly accessible. The Arthur H. Breed, Jr., Freeway (Interstate Highway 580), prominent in this 1987 view, played an important role in the development of Dublin, Pleasanton, and Livermore. Courtesy, Pacific Aerial Surveys

CHAPTER 7

A SPLENDOR OF DIVERSITY

Diversity and change may be the keys to Alameda County's future success. Certainly both were being supported and encouraged in the 1970s and 1980s. Virtually every community has been affected by the shift to a retail, service, and information society, and the people of the county have met the challenge with enthusiasm and ingenuity.

At one time, four-fifths of the acreage of Alameda County was devoted to raising grain, fruits, vegetables, grapes, flowers, livestock, and poultry. Techniques developed here stimulated agricultural production in the Central Valley and Sonoma, Napa, and other counties. Smokestack industries next took the forefront and once again Alameda County was renowned for its productivity.

Today's residents are proving themselves equally skillful at adapting to the computer age. Not only workers but also industries have moved from metropolitan to outlying areas. Firms from nearby Silicon Valley are also expanding into Alameda County.

MAKING CONNECTIONS

Mass transit facilities improved dramatically in 1972, as the nation's first fully computerized light rail system began operations. Twenty years from concept to realization, the Bay Area Rapid Transit District (BART) is headquartered in Oakland. Utilizing a combination of elevated and underground tracks, the extensive system services Alameda, Contra Costa, and San Francisco counties.

The Port of Oakland continued to be an asset to the entire county, exchanging properties and services with other agencies in ways that saved millions of taxpayers' dollars. As BART prepared to sink its $133-million transit tube (the world's largest and deepest) beneath the bay, the port commissioners granted an easement to route the tube along Seventh Street in return for BART's agreement to demolish the old Southern Pacific Mole and fill the adjoining 140 acres with the debris acquired in excavating the system's subway sections. The 12 additional berths constructed atop the fill increased the port's capacity by 80 percent.

In 1962 the commissioners donated the 105 acres of land (acquired through an ingenious swap with the East Bay Regional Park District) on which the Oakland-Alameda County Coliseum was built. They later leased 620 acres of shoreline and San Leandro Bay to the EBRPD (for one dollar a year) for public recreational use. The port has transformed Embarcadero Cove into a modern recreation and entertainment center, and is engaged in a $100-million beautification and reconstruction of Jack London Square.

On September 15, 1962, more than half a million people attended the opening of the new $20-million Metropolitan Oakland International Airport. Much as the Port of Oakland had pioneered commercial aviation, it was soon to dominate shipping in the Bay Area. Although lacking any actual clients, the port spent $600,000 upgrading facilities to handle

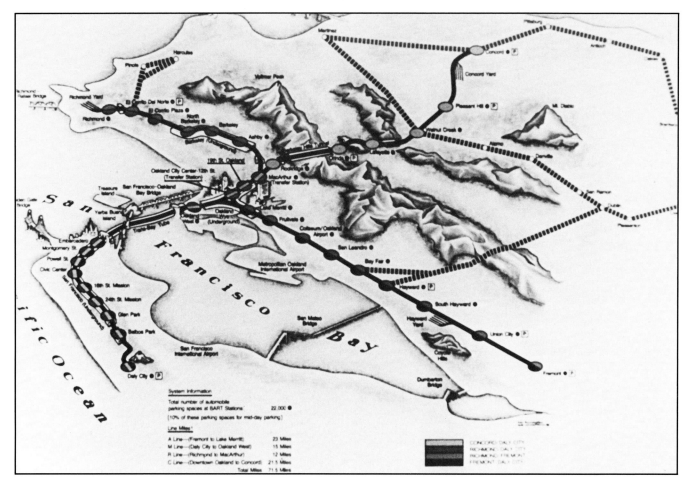

Above: The map of the Bay Area Rapid Transit System demonstrates how Alameda County, and Oakland in particular, serves as the transportation hub of the Bay Area. All lines north, south, east, and west pass through Oakland. Courtesy, Bay Area Rapid Transit

Right: The nation's first totally computerized light-rail system, Bay Area Rapid Transit (BART), started operations in 1972. BART is headquartered in Oakland near the "crossroads" of the system. Courtesy, Bay Area Rapid Transit

the ships of the future. This prescience was justified on September 27, 1962, when Sea-Land Service, Inc., inaugurated intercoastal containership operations as the SS *Elizabethport,* the world's largest freighter, docked at the Outer Harbor Terminal.

The Port of Oakland, second-largest container port in the United States, has become one of the largest and most productive municipally owned enterprises on the West Coast. Adding three billion dollars a year to the local economy, the port offers some of the best commercial containerized shipping facilities in the world, and is directly or indirectly the county's largest employer.

THE CONTEMPORARY COMMUNITIES

In the 1970s the pace of change accelerated. New waves of immigration, including many refugees, enriched the cultural mix while placing additional demands on community services. Lured by fast freeway and BART access, open spaces, and more affordable housing, commuters flocked to the outlying areas of the county to buy homes. New communities proliferated around the regional shopping centers that came with suburbanization.

At the same time, blue-collar workers lost their jobs as food-processing plants shut down and manufacturers of steel, cars, and diesel engines moved to Asia or other parts of the U.S. where land and labor were cheaper. Civic leaders in both the metropolitan and suburban areas were forced to rethink their visions for the future. Downtown facelifts were begun in virtually every community in the county.

The city of Fremont was planned in anticipation of what lay ahead. Taking a leaf from the book of their future city's namesake, John C. Frémont (who once attempted to buy the Mission San Jose grounds for his own home), the planners first surveyed the area's resources and prospects. Their comprehensive zoning code provided cluster housing with shared green spaces; a Civic Center including not only areas for government functions but also recreational parklands; and 7,000 acres set aside for industrial use. The city got an economic boost when General Motors and Toyota formed a partnership to produce automobiles

under both names in the retooled Chevrolet plant. Encompassing nearly 100 square miles, Fremont is the largest city in land area in the county.

Pleasanton also found the transition to a postindustrial, suburban society relatively painless. While some have mourned the reduction of acreage devoted to farming, the community has acquired extensive business and office parks on the perimeter without sacrificing the congenial qualities of the familiar downtown area.

For the communities that grew and shrank with a factory economy the transition has been more difficult. But residents have faced this challenge with imagination and courage.

By pioneering live-work zoning, Emeryville has converted old warehouse and factory buildings to a center for artists and designers (a complex of home-office-studio units) and a center for bio-tech research and development. New construction includes high-rise condominiums and the Watergate complex of apartments, shops, and restaurants with an adjacent harbor for pleasure craft. The funky sculpture of the Emeryville mudflats is being

The Port of Oakland won its competition with San Francisco in 1968 to become home to Japan's six major container shipping corporations, the Bay Area's dominant port, and the West Coast's largest container facility. Today the Port of Oakland owns and manages over 19 miles of shoreline properties. Courtesy, Board of Port Commissioners, Port of Oakland

Superior court Judge Lionel Wilson became Oakland's first black mayor in 1977 and was serving his third term in 1988. Wilson's election broke a long-held white Republican claim to the office. Courtesy, Office of the Mayor, City of Oakland

residential and commercial development. Alameda's excellent marina facilities have afforded it recognition as a center of pleasure boating in Northern California. In 1982, after 12 years of grappling with the problem of erosion, the East Bay Regional Park District succeeded in converting the former Neptune Beach amusement park area into Crown Memorial State Beach—the largest and most heavily used swimming beach on San Francisco Bay.

Since early settlement, Alameda County has been blessed with ethnic, cultural, and philosophical diversity. Perhaps nowhere is this more evident than in modern-day Livermore. Here local cowboy-ranchers work alongside nuclear physicists of the Lawrence Livermore Laboratory. At the impressive new Shiva-Vishnu Temple nearby, two *pandits* (scholars of the Sanskrit language and the ancient Vedic religious texts) minister to the Bay Area's nearly 3,000 Hindu families.

Hayward, too, reflects its cosmopolitan heritage. Kumiko Fujii, honored for her far-flung community involvement as Distinguished Citizen of the Year in 1972, became the first woman president of the AC Transit Board of Directors three years later. Hayward's Kumu Hula Association of Northern California sponsors an annual hula contest that attracts entrants from Hawaii as well as the mainland. From 1966-1972 Hayward was the host to annual pow wows sponsored by the United Bay Area American Indian Council. The annual rodeo and parade celebrates a Hispanic tradition carried on since rancho days, and the Portuguese Festival has been held each year for more than a century.

In Oakland, which has become a veritable melting pot, a variety of cultures and races are working together to help move the city into the 21st century while retaining the charm and legacy of the city's historic neighborhoods. Working with both government redevelopment funds and private capital, the Oakland rejuvenation projects include Chinatown; Old Oakland, a complex of renovated 19th-century Victorians bounded by 8th, 10th, Broadway, and Washington streets; City Square; the Rotunda, a 1913 Neo-classical landmark; and the Civic Center project, which has reformed downtown Oakland into a viable retail/con-

removed to make way for a wildlife sanctuary.

New technologies have made it possible to open the waterfront to recreational, commercial, and residential use. San Leandro is planning 2,000 new homes along the shoreline beside existing golf courses and restaurants. The Davis Street redevelopment project will transform old factory sites into a mile-long stretch of new offices, warehouses, and apartments.

Change has also come to the city of Alameda, where the planned communities of Harbor Bay Isle and Marina Village offer both

vention area. The old Hotel Oakland, long vacant, has been rehabilitated to provide apartments for senior citizens on the upper floors, while the palatial ground floor is being developed for commercial use. Likewise, the art deco Paramount Theater has been refurbished to serve as a center for the performing arts.

A new cadre of leaders took the reins in the mid-1970s. The Gannett chain bought the *Oakland Tribune* and installed Robert F. Maynard as editor. Former superior court Judge Lionel Wilson, first elected mayor in 1977, was serving his third term in 1988.

Oakland's civic leaders continue to woo domestic and Pacific Rim investors and to encourage the interest of the movie industry in shooting films in Oakland. Both financial and social problems are pressing; such cultural assets as the Oakland Ballet are struggling to survive without the customary city support. Led by influential citizens like UC Professor Harry Edwards and the Reverend J. Alfred Smith of the Allen Temple Baptist Church, coalitions of volunteers are attacking the problems of inner-city turbulence.

Neighboring cities have also experienced both the anxiety and the exuberance associated with change. Led by Eugene Norman "Gus" Newport, mayor from 1979 to 1987, Berkeley maintained its place in the forefront of social and philosophical experimentation. U.S. Congressman Ron Dellums, a Berkeley resident, ably represents his constituents in Washington. Among other achievements, Mayor Loni Hancock has succeeded in finalizing a long-deadlocked West Berkeley development that will combine businesses with residential and work space for artists and also ensure the continued presence of an adjacent biotechnology firm. Former activists, in the politically neutral role of restaurateurs, have helped to give Berkeley a reputation as a center for the nouvelle California cuisine. Sport fishing, an important economic factor in the community, continues to thrive at the Berkeley Marina.

High in the hills of the UC campus, the cyclotron built using knowledge gained from research projects of World War II is being used in the treatment of more than 150 cancer patients a year, and scientists are perfecting smaller cyclotrons for installation in hospitals.

In field tests, University of California research projects have demonstrated the safety of the controversial "ice minus" bacteria for agricultural use. As if to demonstrate that the old spirit survives, law students recently staged a sit-in at Boalt Hall to protest university hiring policies.

ENJOYING THE GARDEN

Amid the serious urban pressures that accompany growth, the people of Alameda County still find time to relax.

The county offers a wide spectrum of recreational choices. The Livermore-Amador Valley Symphony has delighted central- and south-county subscribers for more than 20 years. The Berkeley Symphony is highly regarded for its renditions of 20th-century music, while the Berkeley Repertory Theater, in its more than 20 years of performances, has built a loyal following. UC's Museum of Modern Art and Pacific Film Archive are nationally recognized, as is the Judah L. Magnes Memorial Museum, named for the Oakland-born Jewish leader who became the first chancellor of the Hebrew University in Jerusalem and proposed a binational state with parity between Arabs and Jews.

One of the county's most significant architectural projects is the Oakland Museum. The collections of three earlier museums became the nuclei of its three divisions: the Oakland Public Museum (History), the Oakland Art Gallery (Art), and the Snow Museum (Natural History). Resembling a modern Babylonian ziggurat, with its hanging gardens, reflecting pools, and sculptured patios, the museum attracts visitors from around the world.

During the 1960s the voters approved a $25.5-million bond issue for a stadium and arena complex. The Oakland-Alameda County Coliseum was completed in 1966.

All Alameda County watched proudly as the Oakland A's won the World Series not only in 1972, but also in 1973 and 1974. The Golden State Warriors won the 1975 National Basketball Association Championship. When the Oakland Raiders became 1977's Super Bowl champs, Oakland exulted in becoming one of only two cities to have championship

teams in all three sports.

In March 1987 the whole Bay Area enjoyed elaborate pyrotechnic displays celebrating the 50th anniversary of the San Francisco-Oakland Bay Bridge. The following July citizens similarly celebrated the reinstallation of the Necklace of Lights around Lake Merritt, which had been darkened since the World War II blackouts.

Perhaps the most distinctive features of the garden that is Alameda are the regional parks. Faced with the imminent development of large wilderness tracts, Contra Costa and the balance of Alameda counties voted to join the East Bay Regional Park District. Now some 63,000 acres in size, the district includes both hilltop and shoreline parks, and is currently building trails between them—a heritage of wilderness areas, open space, interpretive programs, and recreation for Bay Area residents that is unmatched anywhere in the United States. The expansion was accomplished during the tenures of General Director William Penn Mott, Jr., and his successor, Richard C. Trudeau, with the support of board member and later President Robert Gordon Sproul, president emeritus of the University of California.

Interest and concern for the future of the

Left: Reggie Jackson's heroics on the baseball diamond contributed to the Oakland Athletics' three consecutive World Series Championships (1973-1975). The A's were the first team to bring a professional sports championship to the Bay Area. Jackson returned to Oakland in 1987 for his final year as an active player. Courtesy, Oakland Athletics Baseball Company

Facing page, top: The Oakland-Alameda County Coliseum, completed in 1966, includes a 53,000-seat outdoor stadium, a 15,500-seat enclosed arena, and a 48,000-square-foot exhibit hall. The facility hosts the annual Virginia Slims Tennis Tournament and is home to the Oakland A's and the Golden State Warriors. Courtesy, Oakland History Room, Oakland Public Library

Facing page, bottom: Mark McGwire's 49 homeruns renewed interest in the Oakland Athletics in 1987. McGwire's exploits earned him American League rookie-of-the-year honors. Courtesy, Oakland Athletics Baseball Company

The Lawrence Hall of Science on the UC Berkeley campus has been one of Alameda County's most popular museums. Life-like exhibits, such as this Apatosaurus being befriended by Michael Gasten of Antioch, continue to educate the public. Courtesy, Oakland Tribune

bay also intensified during the 1960s. Kay Kerr, wife of the president of the University of California, organized the "Save the Bay" campaign, whose study led to the formation of the San Francisco Bay Conservation and Development Commission (BCDC) with authority over all filling of the bay. Other private and public groups pressed for the establishment of a wildlife refuge in the South Bay, and in 1972 Congress established the San Francisco Bay National Wildlife Refuge, which was dedicated with an Amtrak train tour through the old railroad community of Drawbridge.

Volunteers continued their efforts to restore both natural and man-made attractions in the 1980s. Following the "Restoring the Earth" conference at the UC Berkeley campus in January 1988, several organized groups began work to preserve, enhance, and restore Sausal, Strawberry, and Alameda creeks.

Recreational passenger trains (powered by both steam and diesel locomotives) returned to the Niles Canyon in May 1988. The old Southern Pacific tracks were repaired and rebuilt by members of the Pacific Locomotive Association, using volunteer labor and donated funds. The club had previously offered public rides on the antique rolling stock at Point Richmond.

Alameda County today, like the rest of Earth's garden, faces challenges that are mind-boggling. Yet residents of the area have long seen diversity as a potential advantage, and change as a challenge to be dealt with. That spirit has kept Alameda County in the lead for generations, and that—coupled with a central geographic location—promises that Alameda County's position as a crossroads will continue with its residents helping to show the world the way to the future.

" Old Number Four," the oldest of Tilden Park's two steam locomotives, cele- brated its 30th anniversary of carrying passengers on the park's Redwood Valley Railway in June 1982. Courtesy, Oakland Tribune

Planted in the 1880s, the hop fields of Pleasanton were the largest in the state by 1900. Companies located as far away as London, England, bought the crops. More than 1,500 workers were required to harvest the hops in September. Courtesy, Amador-Livermore Valley Historical Society

PARTNERS IN PROGRESS

With a romantic Spanish and Mexican heritage, 733-square-mile Alameda County, created March 25, 1853, from portions of two counties—Contra Costa and Santa Clara—has achieved a population growth of more than one million in its 135 years.

The 1853 population of some 3,000 included Oakland's 200 to 300 squatters near the foot of Broadway, Spanish Dons and their families on their sprawling land grants, the native Indian population, commercial fishermen, and disenchanted gold seekers who had returned from the Mother Lode to engage in ranching or commerce.

The county was essentially agricultural then. Now the Association of Bay Area Governments (ABAG), in its "Projections '87," foresees a distinct shift in emphasis to high-technology office and service-related industries for the 20-year period 1985-2005. With this change will come marked population and employment shifts, largely to Fremont and the Livermore-Amador Valley areas. The estimated population for Alameda County in the year 2005 is 1.414 million. Over the 20-year ABAG projection, it is forecast that 40 percent of the nine-county Bay Region's growth will occur in Alameda and Santa Clara counties,

and just in excess of 50 percent of the region's jobs will be located there.

Since its founding Alameda County has had many county seats: Alvarado, San Leandro, Brooklyn, and lastly Oakland. The Port of Oakland boasts the largest containerized port, in physical size, on the West Coast. It ranks among the top 10 in the nation and the top 20 in the world. Its modern airport handles 200 passenger flights daily, in direct connection with 210 U.S. cities, and served 3.8 million passengers in 1986. Today Oakland's diverse population is two-thirds black, Hispanic, and Asian, and 34 languages are spoken. The changes in Alameda County, fifth largest among the state's 58, have been profound since Francisco Ortega first sighted the southern reaches of San Francisco Bay from the mountainous spine of San Mateo County on November 2, 1769.

The organizations whose stories are detailed on the following pages have chosen to support this important literary and civic project. They illustrate the variety of ways in which individuals and their businesses have contributed to the growth and development of Alameda County.

ALAMEDA COUNTY HISTORICAL SOCIETY

Many refer to Superior Court Judge Redmond C. Staats, Jr. (left), as the founding president of the Alameda County Historical Society since Judge Donovan's life was cut short before he could complete its organization and prepare an agenda of activities. Here Judge Staats receives a lifetime membership plaque in 1981 from Edward T. Schnaar, another past president.

History is the witness that testifies to the passing of time; it illumines reality, vitalizes memory, provides guidance in daily life, and brings us tidings of antiquity.

—Cicero

The Alameda County Historical Society held what was described as its organization meeting on March 30, 1965, and elected Superior Court Judge Augustin "Mike" Donovan, president; Superior Court Judge Richard H. Chamberlain, vice-president; and Henrietta H. Perry, longtime curator of the old Oakland Museum, executive secretary.

Unfortunately Donovan died on October 19, 1965, hardly before the newly born society, dedicated to Clio, could complete organization and prepare an agenda of activities. A founding meeting was held on approximately June 5, 1966, and, soon thereafter, Superior Court Judge Redmond C. Staats, Jr., took over as president. The first elected board of directors was seated in 1967, and the *Tribune* of February 9 of that year identified Perry as the society's founder. Charter memberships were closed as of December 31, 1967. It was made clear that the Alameda County Historical Society "had no connection . . . with one of the same name that existed 30 years ago" that was unincorporated.

According to the files of the old *Quarterlys*, there have been 18 presidents since 1965, including Judge Donovan. (Some have chosen to disregard the 1965 period and date the true start of the society as 1966, identifying Judge Staats as the founding president.) The complete roster of society presidents reads: Donovan, March-October 1965; Staats, 1966-January 1969; Judge Richard H. Chamberlain, 1969-1970; Richard H. McCarthy, 1970-1971; Judge John S. Cooper, 1971-1972; Louis Stein, Jr., 1972-1973; Judge Donald Quayle, 1973-1974; Edward T. Schnarr, 1974-1975; Homer C. Votaw, 1975-1976; Paul A. Brom, 1976-1977; Mrs. Robert H. Swadley, 1977-1978;

Superior Court Judge Augustin "Mike" Donovan was named president of the new Alameda County Historical Society at its organization meeting on March 30, 1965. He died six months later.

Mrs. Frances Buxton, longtime employee of the Oakland Public Library and an expert on the history of the East Bay, was the 18th president of the Alameda County Historical Society.

Leonard Verbarg, 1978-1979; Homer C. Votaw, 1979-1980; Superior Court Judge William McGuinness, 1980-1981; Edward T. Schnarr, 1981-1982; Felton L. Watson, 1982-1983; Mrs. Roy Kiaer, 1983-1984; Jay ver Lee, 1984-1985; State Senator Arthur H. Breed, Jr., 1985-1987; and Frances A. Buxton, 1987-1988. The current president is Elmer Johnson.

Interest in the society was evidently brisk; the records show that what was described as "the first meeting of the society" in June 1966 was attended by 200 and "not even standing room was left."

The long list of distinguished speakers who have addressed the society and the topics discoursed upon include William Sturm, "The Hotels of Oakland"; Dr. Peter Conmy, two appearances to discuss Oakland's Pardee family and Francis Marion "Bora" Smith; John Sandoval, Southern Alameda County's peerless historian, "The Story of Hayward" and "The Adams of Eden"; Father William Abeloe, "The History of Mission San Jose"; the Reverend Maynard J. Geiger, Mission Santa Barbara archivist, "Father Junipero Serra"; Louis Stein, Jr., "Old Memories of Berkeley"; and bestselling author Richard Dillon, "Wells Fargo Detective—The Life of James B. Hume."

EDEN HOSPITAL MEDICAL CENTER

This tiny newborn infant, held by one of the registered nurses at Eden Hospital Medical Center, is one of the 53,000 babies which have been born at Eden during its 33-year history. The hospital now serves a population of 600,000 in southern Alameda and Contra Costa counties.

Eden Hospital Medical Center, Castro Valley, California. Employing more than 1,000 health care professionals, Eden is a community hospital governed by a publicly elected board of directors. More than 400 highly skilled physicians care for their patients at the 231-bed hospital.

In concert with the district it serves, Eden Hospital Medical Center has grown and changed as the needs of the area's 600,000 residents have also changed.

Conveniently located near two major transportation corridors, Eden is the regional trauma center for southern Alameda County.

The hospital's vital statistics tally shows that some 53,000 babies have been born at Eden during its three-decade history. During 1987, 1,084 babies were born at Eden and a total of 7,550 patients underwent treatment at the hospital.

Dev Mahadevan, the hospital's president and chief executive officer, was quick to recognize the need for a shift in emphasis in the services offered

by Eden. Commenting on the change in name from Eden Hospital to Eden Hospital Medical Center, Mahadevan observed that "Eden is now more than a place where people come when they are ill or hurt; it is a place for people to come when they need information about staying well and being healthy. It is now a regional health care facility. Responsive to change, Eden is starting to learn how to care for an older population as the population it serves ages."

Eden Hospital Medical Center, which had been a community goal since 1939, grew closer to reality when the voters approved formation of the 60-square-mile Eden Township Hospital District in 1948. A year later they voted for a construction bond issue. The hospital opened November 15, 1954. Essentially, Eden is a 231-bed general acute care hospital with some 1,200 employees. New components are added and new technologies adopted to keep pace with changes in medicine and in Eden's community.

A $3.5-million Intensive Care Unit opened in 1987. Eden now

supports two senior housing developments, Landmark Villa, a 96-unit retirement community in Hayward, and Baywood Court, a 251-unit development in Castro Valley, which offers three levels of care—independent living, assisted living, and a skilled nursing facility—on a single site.

Given a logical opportunity to expand at the right time, Eden purchased neighboring Laurel Grove Hospital with its 78 beds and 125 employees.

Other services offered by Eden include an entire floor of the hospital devoted to women's health services, a burn care center, an extensive variety of rehabilitation programs, and an eating disorders unit, as well as a host of specialized services for cancer patients and their families as a Community Cancer Center.

MOTHER'S CAKE & COOKIE CO.

N.M. "Mique" Wheatley, founder of Mother's Cake & Cookie Co., is shown at approximately the turn of the century selling newspapers at San Francisco's Market and Kearny streets.

The Reverend Horatio Alger (1832-1899), an American novelist who specialized in writing books about newsboys or bootblacks who through hard work and self-reliance achieved riches, must have had Mique Wheatley specifically in mind as the archetypal hero. For N.M. Wheatley (he didn't like his first name, Noah, and Mique, pronounced Mike, was the way his French mother spelled it) rose, through sheer enterprise and hard work, from a hometown and foreign newspaper vendor at San Francisco's Market and Kearny streets to president of Oakland's multimillion-dollar Mother's Cake & Cookie Co. Today its five band ovens bake more than 2 billion cookies per year.

Leapfrogging ahead approximately 69 years from the 1914 origins of Mother's Cake & Cookie Co. to today in order to put this remarkable success

story in the proper perspective, the firm underwent two major changes in ownership in recent years. First, in May 1983, Generale Biscuit of France, the third-largest cookie group in the world with bakeries in some 30 European countries, acquired the Oakland firm. Mother's immediately became a distributor in the United States of Generale Biscuit's premier "LU" brand. Then, in 1986, a controlling interest in Generale Biscuit of France was acquired by the BSN Group of Paris, a major player worldwide in the food industry.

Projected gross sales for 1988 for Mother's are tabbed at $120 million. Michel M. Laverne took over the presidency in 1983. From being a staunch independent, Mother's Cake & Cookie Co. had, overnight you might say, joined the worldwide club of movers and shakers in the baking world, though its origins were humble.

Wheatley's father was a stonemason with a family of 13 in Beckingham, England. He was eight years old when his father died, and it became necessary, since the family was in difficult circumstances, to send Mique and one of his brothers to Woodsley, Ontario, Canada. There they were placed in foster homes under agency supervision. They worked on farms in the summer and went to school in the winter. One report dealing with Wheatley read, in part, that he was "somewhat troublesome and was dismissed from a former situation for remaining out late at night . . ."

Young Wheatley toiled in the Canadian summers and hit the books in the winter for about five years; then he ran away. He made his way west, working as a blacksmith and in Canadian lumber camps. He reached San Francisco about 1895. There, at some 17 years of age, he entered the newspaper business. First he had a two-wheel cart; then he worked up to a four-wheel cart.

The newspaper business apparently held Wheatley's exclusive atten-

N.M. Wheatley was so taken by some vanilla cookies that a San Francisco couple peddled from a covered basket that he made a deal to get the recipe and started a bakery. Wheatley made deliveries in a rig with a horse named Vanilla (above). The cookie business was so successful that Vanilla had to be put out to pasture, succeeded by a Model T Ford. Here (below) Wheatley, who did a little of everything, polishes up the delivery truck.

tion for nearly two decades, until he was attracted by an elderly couple who passed by every day, carrying a covered basket. He struck up a conversation, learned there were home-baked vanilla cookies in the basket, tried one and liked it, and decided on the spot to make a deal to purchase the rights to the recipe.

The date was April 1914, and Wheatley was going to enter the cookie baking business and say "good-bye" to

Quality-assurance men ride tricycles to keep an eye on the various controls on the band ovens, some of them the length of a football field, at Mother's Cake & Cookie Co. in Oakland. Here, in 1957, little Gayle Wheatley, daughter of Floyd Wheatley who in 1955 assumed the presidency of the firm, gets a cookie from fellow tricyclist George Stevens while Floyd Wheatley looks on.

than 20 million pounds of flour and 15 million pounds of sugar are consumed in a year. The plant even makes its own powdered sugar. Ordinarily two or three shifts a day are worked.

Too bad Mique didn't live to see it all. Censured at an early age for "remaining out late at night," he survived to create a thriving business doing precisely that. His one-man plant evolved into one with a work force of 350 in Oakland, producing 60 different cookies distributed in 14 states—including Alaska, Hawaii, and Texas—through a sales force of more than 300.

newspaper vending. San Francisco's 1906 earthquake and fire impelled Wheatley to opt for an East Bay location now that he was going to invest in something more permanent than a cart. His first small, one-man plant was at 1115-12th Avenue in Oakland. There he toiled all night baking cookies in a three-square-foot oven. His nightly output was about 2,000 cookies, or 15 boxes, each containing 13.5 dozen cookies. The price? One dollar a box. Wheatley's vanilla cookies were an overnight success. He needed help and hired a young woman. Romance ultimately flourished amidst work in the little bakery, and the newly hired assistant became Wheatley's wife, Leopoldine. After his death in 1955, she assumed the chairmanship of the firm until their son, Floyd, succeeded her.

Money was scarce, so Mique Wheatley rented a horse and wagon.

The name of the horse, appropriately, was Vanilla. Later Model T Fords outdistanced Vanilla.

By 1922 the operation needed more space, and a much larger plant at 1148 East 18th Street was acquired. To swing the deal, though, Wheatley had to sell his house and even the piano to muster the necessary funds. In 1949 it was moving time again—this time to an 11-acre site at 810-81st Avenue. There five band ovens—three of them 300 feet long—turn out about one million cookies in an hour and a half. Dough is mixed in one-ton batches, and more

Michel M. Laverne took over the presidency of Mother's Cake & Cookie Co. in 1983, when the firm was acquired by Generale Biscuit of France. Subsequently a majority interest in Generale Biscuit was purchased by the BSN Group of Paris.

WASHINGTON HOSPITAL HEALTHCARE SYSTEM

Fremont's Washington Hospital was dedicated on November 22, 1958. Ed Enos, former member of the hospital board, is the speaker.

It was the mid-1940s, and America was living the glory and the tragedy of World War II. It would be years before five small communities would band together to create Fremont. But the time was right for the creation of a local hospital, and public-minded citizens of southern Alameda County organized a campaign to do just that.

Washington Township Hospital District was created in 1948. The district represents an area of about 124 square miles, including what is today the cities of Fremont, Newark, Union City, and a portion of Hayward. It is governed through a publicly elected five-member board of directors.

The construction of Washington Hospital, financed through a publicly-approved bond issue, was completed in the late 1950s, and the 156-bed hospital opened its doors on November 22, 1958. Situated adjacent to a cauliflower field on what was then Santos Road, Washington Hospital soon became a permanent fixture on the Fremont skyline.

As the Tri-City area grew from a small, rural community to a major suburban hub of the south San Francisco Bay Area, Washington Hospital expanded services and programs to meet the health care needs of its citizens. Chief executive officer and administrator Richard M. Warren joined the

hospital staff in 1969, just in time to oversee a major expansion program completed five years later that increased the hospital's bed capacity to 265 and expanded ancillary services.

During the expansion program, the Lester S. Whitaker Pavilion, named for the hospital district's first chairman of the board, was constructed to provide additional space. Today the Whitaker Pavilion operates as a 29-bed Mental Health Unit.

Later an expanded Physical Therapy Department was added, as well as a Computed Tomography (CT) Head and Body Scanner Suite. An upgraded emergency department sees 40,000 emergency cases per year, and a helipad has been constructed to facilitate emergency patient transfers.

The cardiac services program began in 1985 and now features the Thomas E. Lowden Medical Imaging Laboratory, a cardiac surgery suite for open-heart surgery, and a cardiac rehabilitation program for patients following surgery or other cardiac incident.

In addition, Washington Hospital offers special services that include renal dialysis, outpatient surgery, crisis intervention, and expanded maternity services that deliver 2,000 new residents each year.

Since 1984 Washington Hospital's services have expanded to include the Washington Stanford Radiation Oncology Center; three urgent care walk-in clinics located in Fremont, Warm Springs, and Newark; a freestanding birth center; and the Washington Outpatient Surgery Center.

Today the Washington Hospital Healthcare System offers the citizens of the Tri-City area convenient, affordable, and quality health care, as it has since the district was formed more than 30 years ago.

Today Washington Hospital, a 265-bed acute care facility, serves the communities of Fremont, Newark, Union City, and South Hayward.

SWADLEY ENTERPRISES

Robert Hunter Swadley, vice-president of Swadley Enterprises.

Bernadine Hatch Swadley, president of Swadley Enterprises.

Swadley Enterprises, a family organization formed to handle the couple's personal affairs, is the creation of Bernadine Hatch Swadley and her husband, Robert Hunter Swadley, both of whom can trace their lineage to the American Revolution. Longtime Oakland residents, they are both extremely active in civic affairs.

Bernadine Swadley, a fourth-generation Californian, is president of Swadley Enterprises; her husband is vice-president. She is honorary state regent, Daughters of the American Revolution; past regent of the Piedmont Chapter; past DAR national officer of the Vice-Regents Club; member of the National DAR Vice-Chairmen's Club; past state president of the Colonial Dames of America; member of the Mayflower Society; past president and state officer of the Daughters of American Colonists; recipient of the Sons of the American Revolution Martha Washington medal; life member and state officer of the Children of the American Revolution; and a member of the Magna Charta Dames.

Robert Swadley is a life member of the Children of the American Revolution; past state officer and adviser of the State C.A.R. Board; life member of the Sons of the American Revolution; and past state president and vice-president, Western District, and trustee and alternate trustee.

A native of Tennessee, he earned a teacher's degree, served in the Air Corps during World War II, and later entered the sales executive and consulting fields. He is extremely active in Episcopal church work and was a director of the Episcopal Homes Foundation. He is also active and has held administrative posts in such organizations as Rotary International; district governor, 1981-1982, of the Lake View Club and the Lake Chabot Golf Club; president of the Oakland Salvation Army; the Boy Scouts of America; president of the Oakland YMCA; YMCA Man of the Year in 1960; and the American Red Cross. He is also a Paul Harris Fellow.

Bernadine Swadley is past president and chairperson of the Landmarks Committee of the Alameda County Historical Society; secretary and first female president of the Oakland-South Alameda County Red Cross Chapter; founder and past president of The Skyline Garden Club; has served 27 years on the board of the Oakland Visiting Nurses Association; is past state president of Beta Sigma Phi; and is the author of "My California Family." Her educational career led to a degree in art, and on occasion she worked as an architectural draftsman. During World War II her business career included a stint as credit manager.

THE TRIBUNE

Back in the days when Oakland's Ninth Street between Broadway and Washington was a very stylish location, the Oakland Daily Tribune *printed its first edition on February 21, 1874, at 468 Ninth Street.*

On February 21, 1874, a four-page newspaper appeared on the streets of Oakland. It sold for five cents and had a paid circulation of 1,000. Benet A. Dewes and editor George B. Staniford called their new publication the *Oakland Daily Tribune.*

In January 1875 the *Tribune* moved to new quarters at 911 Broadway, and in July 1876 William E. Dargie bought out the paper's original owners and added the wire services of the Associated Press.

The *Tribune* soon found it necessary to move again to larger offices, and on October 1, 1877, relocated to 12th and Franklin streets. By August 1891 the paper had added bureaus in New York and Chicago, and the name *Oakland Tribune* was officially adopted. By the early 1900s the *Tribune* had also hired Jack Gunin, one of the first full-

time newspaper photographers in the West.

On June 28, 1906, the enterprise once again moved, to Eighth and

Franklin streets, occupying the lower floors of the Golden West Hotel, and the editorial direction of the paper was turned over to managing editor John Conners. On November 3, 1915, former congressman Joseph R. Knowland took control of the *Tribune,* writing in an editorial, "it is perfectly understood that what it (the paper) does, rather than what it promises, will determine the full measure of its worth."

The *Tribune's* comprehensive coverage of World War I resulted in rapid circulation growth, and on March 25, 1918, the paper moved to its present location at 13th and Franklin streets. The familiar Tribune Tower was erected in 1923 where all business offices were relocated. The original building has since been converted to the press room and other production departments.

During the 1920s the *Tribune* was instrumental in encouraging many civic reforms in the East Bay. It was also actively involved in initiating the city manager-city council form of government in Oakland, as well as helping to

Shown is a facsimile of page one of volume one, number one, of the Oakland Daily Tribune *dated February 21, 1874. The newspaper is still going strong today. Column one of the initial 1874 issue extolled the virtues of the sign painted for the Castro Meat Market and spoke disparagingly of competitive "vile daubs."*

Around the turn of the century this horse-drawn carriage served as a means of advertising for the Tribune. The sign on the side of the vehicle proclaimed the Tribune *as a printer and a book binder.*

lowing Senator Knowland's death in 1974, his son became editor and publisher.

Young Joseph Knowland ran the *Tribune* for three years, fighting rising costs and increasing competition from San Francisco and suburban dailies. In 1977, after 62 years of family own-

Shown here are members of the Knowland family who controlled the Tribune for 62 years. From left are the late Joseph R. Knowland, who acquired the paper in 1915; his son, the late U.S. Senator William F. Knowland, who assumed the reins as publisher in 1964 when his father died; and the senator's wife, Helen.

establish the Port of Oakland and the East Bay Municipal Utility District.

When Joe Knowland died in 1964, his son, the late U.S. Senator William F. Knowland, became editor and publisher. The newspaper saturated Oakland and began circulating widely in the sprawling East Bay suburbs. Fol-

ership, the Knowlands sold the *Tribune* to Combined Communications, a multimedia corporation. In 1979 the Gannett Corporation merged with Combined Communications and acquired the *Tribune.*

Nationally respected journalist Robert C. Maynard was appointed editor in August 1979. The following November, while continuing to publish the afternoon *Tribune,* the morning edition was converted to a commuter-oriented 10-cent street-sales-only edition called *Eastbay Today.*

In 1981 Maynard became the *Tribune*'s publisher, and the following year the morning and afternoon news-

papers were combined into one morning paper renamed the *Tribune.*

In April 1983 Maynard reached an agreement with Gannett Corporation for the purchase of the *Tribune.* A new board of directors was installed, and the *Tribune* once again became an independently owned newspaper.

Today, with more than 900 employees and nearly 350,000 readers, the *Tribune* maintains its position as the largest daily newspaper in the greater East Bay by providing comprehensive world and national news combined with the best zoned local coverage every day.

In addition, the *Tribune*'s unique complement of columnists and weekly feature sections such as "Money Monday," "Lifestyle," "Wednesday Food," "Weekend!," and "Sports" help make the good life even better for its readers.

With a history of service dating back to 1874, the *Tribune* is truly the greater East Bay's greater newspaper.

Robert C. Maynard, veteran newspaperman with a Washington, D.C., background, was appointed editor of the Tribune *in August 1979, and became, in addition, the publisher two years later. He is photographed against the landmark Tribune Tower and adjacent* Tribune *publishing plant. Photo by Kenneth Green*

MOREHOUSE FOODS, INC.

George F. Latter, former railroad passenger agent, established such a record selling mustard that the founding Morehouse family assigned him to open the new Emeryville Branch of Morehouse Foods in 1919.

Harold Latter, fresh from service in World War I, came to Emeryville to help his father, George, as the first full-time employee. He is the father of David Latter, the current president of Morehouse Foods, Inc. A fourth-generation Latter heads the Los Angeles branch.

Did you think that the days of the thrifty, well-managed family enterprises had succumbed to complicated corporate mergers and to wide-ranging conglomerates? The tradition continues in 89-year-old Morehouse Foods, Inc., which specializes in the manufacture of prepared mustards and horseradish.

Headquartered in a modest building at 4221 Hollis Street, Emeryville, and with a branch in Los Angeles, the firm sells some 3.5 million gallons of mustard annually. Add to that 500,000 gallons of horseradish and the manufacture of some 60 private- or house-label mustards for retail firms.

"There is hardly a week that I don't receive an offer to sell or merge," David Latter, the president and sole owner, observes. "Our firm is among the top half-dozen mustard producers in the nation."

Mustard, Latter points out, is no Johnny-Come-Lately. It has been cultivated for perhaps 2,500 years, and there are references to it in the Bible and in Shakespeare's writings. The Emeryville

plant gets its mustard seed from Western Canada and the horseradish from Tule Lake, California.

The thriving condiment firm was founded in Chicago during the Spanish-American War by Miles O. and Lou H. Morehouse. In 1913 they moved the plant to Los Angeles. In 1919 along came George F. Latter who, a decade before, had been given a year or so to live by his doctors. He met Miles Morehouse at a church function, and Morehouse offered him a job. On his first Northern California swing as a salesman, he sold seven carloads of mustard. He remained with the firm for many years, dying at the age of 86.

The Morehouses were convinced that a Bay Area headquarters was needed. George Latter opened the Emeryville branch on September 1, 1919, in a small, nondescript wooden

This is the modern and enlarged plant of Morehouse Foods, Inc., situated at 4221 Hollis Street in Emeryville as it appeared in 1950. Together with its Los Angeles plant, the firm turns out 3.5 million gallons of mustard annually.

building on the Hollis Street site. In those inchoate years the little firm was hemmed in by saloons, and across the street was the colorful and historic Oakland Trotting Park. At the rear of the property was a popular house of ill-repute that had attained some measure of celebrity; it was peremptorily shut down when the Morehouse firm acquired the property. In due time George Latter's son, Harold, joined him as the only full-time employee. When Miles Morehouse died in 1927, the Latters bought the Emeryville plant and its sales territory.

Ultimately Harold's son, David, the current president, assumed command. His son, David Jr., representing the fourth generation of Latters in the firm, is vice-president and general manager of the Los Angeles plant, which was also acquired by the Latters.

Of course you want to know where that oft-bandied phrase, "couldn't cut the mustard," originated. David Latter credits it to O. Henry who in his "Hearts of the West" wrote: "I looked around and found a proposition that exactly cut the mustard." Does the pungent horseradish figure in literature too? Of course. Samuel Pepys, the Secretary of the British Admiralty, wrote in his famed diary in 1664: "He would needs have me drink a cup of horseradish ale." Morehouse Foods, Inc., does not manufacture horseradish ale.

BOYLE, COWAN & CO., CERTIFIED PUBLIC ACCOUNTANTS

Lawrence S. Timpson, CPA, founded Oakland's pioneer certified public accounting firm in 1924. Built on professional excellence and high-quality personal service, the concern is now known as Boyle, Cowan & Co.

Boyle, Cowan & Co., Certified Public Accountants, traces its history in Oakland to 1924 and is one of the oldest CPA concerns in the city. The foundation upon which it was built is "professional excellence and high-quality personal service to clients."

In fact, a thumbnail acronym summing up the firm's long-term reputation is "SID" representing stability, integrity, and dependability, the partners say.

Lawrence S. Timpson, CPA, founded the original firm years ago—it has been through nine name changes since then—in the year that George Gershwin wrote his "Rhapsody in Blue" and the nation had two female governors, Miriam "Ma" Ferguson of Texas and Nellie Tayloe Ross of Wyoming. The firm's spacious offices are at 1610 Harrison Street, Oakland.

During the late 1950s Martin Huff was one of the partners. He went on to become Oakland City auditor-

controller and then executive officer of the State Franchise Tax Board.

The managing partner is Reed Cowan, CPA, and other partners are William J. Boyle, CPA, who served as managing partner for 29 years and stepped down to ease off a bit; Dennis S. Kaneshiro, CPA; and William E. Moy, CPA. All partners have been promoted from within. Cowan is only the third managing partner in the organization's history. The concern prides itself in participation in community affairs and all the partners are active.

"Early on, the firm saw that data processing would be the wave of the future and is continually upgrading its EDP facilities," Cowan declares. "Portable microcomputers were acquired for field use, and they enhanced our ability to perform audits, reviews, and compilations. In retrospect, many of us feared that with the advent of data processing, some CPAs might be put out of work. Just the reverse proved to be true. The mass of information and paper the new technology provided only increased business."

Both Cowan and Boyle have distinguished careers in many facets of community service. Cowan is also a past vice-president of the California Society of CPAs, was on the board of directors of that organization for seven years, is a past president of the East Bay Chapter of CPAs, and is a past member of the Governing Council of the American Institute of CPAs. Boyle is also a past president of the East Bay CPA Chapter, a past member of the board of directors of the California CPA Society, and won the accolade of local Boss of the Year.

Cowan allows that CPA work is

not all a grinding, meticulous drudgery involving ledgers, journals, credits, and debits. He recalls auditing the accounts of a small town in the wine country. When he got around to the dog catcher, he found the accounts five dollars short. That worthy reached into his pocket and fished out a fiver, an informal way to balance the books. The next year the dog catcher's books were $7.50 over. The man promptly claimed the overage. It was explained it did not work that way; the surplus remained in the vaults.

William J. Boyle, CPA, recently stepped down as managing partner of the Oakland certified public accounting firm of Boyle, Cowan & Co. after 29 years in that position. Boyle still remains with the firm; Reed Cowan, CPA, has assumed the post of managing partner.

INTEL CORPORATION

Intel's Livermore plant.

Intel Corporation in Livermore is an uncommon blend of streamlined high technology at work 24 hours a day, seven days a week, and warm support for the virtues of an old-fashioned "homefolks" life for its employees.

The firm, which is "the largest manufacturer of semiconductor memory components and microcomputer systems in the world," is a billion-dollar business that began with 12 employees and now has some 20,000. Its products and processes are included in such items as personal computers, digital gasoline pumps, computer and engineering systems, automatic teller machines, medical instrumentation, point-of-sale terminals, automotive computers, telecommunications, and factory automation equipment.

From the company's inception in Mountain View in 1968, Intel's founders—Dr. Gordon E. Moore, chairman and chief executive officer, and Dr. Robert N. Noyce, vice-chairman and co-inventor of the integrated circuit—have generally agreed on the firm's emphasis: "When we select a new plant site, our primary concern is finding an area that is conducive to wholesome family life. We look for areas that have low pollution levels, good schools, and are growing at a moderate rate."

In addition, the founders of Intel (an acronym for integrated electronics) have encouraged a small-company atmosphere through the establishment of largely autonomous branch manufacturing plants (the company calls them "Fabs") throughout four western states. It places a premium on such things as teamwork; assuming responsibility; sharing ideas on a one-to-one, first-name basis; and promotion from within wherever possible.

The company pioneered LSI technology (large-scale integrated memory), the placement of thousands of microminiature electronic devices on a tiny silicon chip.

Ted Jenkins, now at the Folsom, California, facility, was the manager when ground breaking for the Livermore Intel plant occurred in late 1972; the plant opened with some 50 employees the following May. Today the plant payroll varies between 500 and 700, and Ken Thompson is the manager.

Cleanliness is the number-one requirement where costly silicon wafers and chips are concerned. When the Livermore plant opened, special "clean" or "white rooms" were introduced. There dust particles are monitored on a per-cubic-meter basis to ensure a sterile environment. Women working there cannot wear makeup and are attired in coveralls called Bunny Suits, booties, and plastic caps.

Outsiders find it fascinating that Intel Corporation's delicate microminiature products are fabricated from silicon—a nonmetallic element (Si 14) that constitutes more than one-quarter of the earth's crust.

Cleanliness is the number one requirement where costly silicon wafers and chips are concerned; consequently, employees must wear "bunny suits" for particle control.

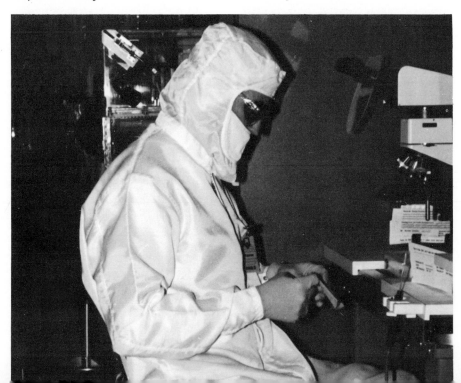

DELOITTE HASKINS & SELLS

Charles E. Schwyn is partner-in-charge of the Deloitte Haskins & Sells accounting offices serving Alameda County. A Big Eight accounting firm, it employs more than 140 professionals in the area and has many large, national firms as clients.

Deloitte Haskins & Sells (DH&S), one of the world's oldest and largest professional services firms and a Big Eight accounting firm, is dedicated to providing quality tax, accounting, auditing, and consulting services to Alameda County clients. The company's Alameda County clients are well served by more than 140 professionals.

DH&S provides professional services to Alameda County organizations of all types, ranging from large and medium-size commercial concerns and governmental entities to emerging businesses. Its major commercial clients include The Clorox Company, Kaiser Cement, KaiserTech, Safeway Stores, Inc., and Shasta Beverages. Emerging business clients include Worlds of Wonder, which has been a client since

its inception in 1985. The firm also serves a number of public-sector clients in Alameda County, such as the Alameda Bureau of Electricity, the Alameda Contra Costa Transit District, the Association of Bay Area Governments, the cities of Hayward and Livermore, the Peralta Community College District, and the Port of Oakland.

DH&S' Oakland office opened in 1974 in the Ordway Building, where it remained until a move to the Kaiser Building in August 1987. The partner-in-charge of the Oakland office, Charles E. "Chuck" Schwyn, demonstrates DH&S' dedication to the Alameda County community on a daily basis. The firm's Alameda County client list includes a variety of not-for-profit organizations, such as the American Red Cross-Oakland, Clausen House, the East Oakland Youth Development Foundation, and Jubilee West, Inc.

Schwyn serves as the 1987-1988 chairman of the board of the Oakland Chamber of Commerce. He is president of the Junior Center of Art and

Science, and currently serves on the boards of the Oakland Police Activities League, the Oakland Rotary Club, and the Oakland YMCA. Committed to helping the youth of Oakland, Schwyn holds board memberships with the Joe Morgan Youth Foundation and the Marcus A. Foster Educational Institute. "To be able to have an impact on Oakland's youth is a service to Oakland's future," he believes.

Chuck Schwyn's enthusiasm and support for community involvement are contagious; DH&S' East Bay professionals are active in organizations such as the Alameda County Easter Seal Society, the Berkeley Shakespeare Festival, the Oakland Ballet, the Oakland Ensemble Theatre, and the YWCA of Oakland.

Deloitte Haskins & Sells is proud to play a significant role in the Alameda County business community. Says Schwyn, "We look forward to many more years of serving our Alameda County clients and responding to the needs of the community at large."

THE RATCLIFF ARCHITECTS

Creative and progressive in its outlook, yet seasoned by 82 years of experience, The Ratcliff Architects is itself a landmark architecture and planning firm, the oldest in the East Bay. Christopher "Kit" Ratcliff, AIA, carries on a three-generation family tradition in the practice of architecture and was recently named president of the firm. Other principals include Don Kasamoto, AIA; Burns Cadwalader, FAIA; and Syed V. Husain, AIA.

The late Walter H. Ratcliff, Jr., AIA, founded the firm in Berkeley on March 15, 1906, just 34 days before the San Francisco earthquake and fire. Many of his first clients were wealthy San Franciscans fleeing to the East Bay to make their homes in the Berkeley hills. He was Berkeley's city architect during the decade 1910 to 1920, and drafted the city's first housing code and zoning ordinance. In addition, he was the Mills College master plan architect for 24 years and designed its Music Building, which won a national AIA award for design excellence. Carrying on the firm's philosophy and commitment to community and civic activities, Robert Ratcliff, second in the family to become a member of the firm in 1945, was awarded the Benjamin Ide Wheeler Award as Berkeley's Most Valuable Citizen for his contributions both as an architect and an involved citizen. Bob Ratcliff is semiretired now, although he

Gathered around a work table at The Ratcliff Architects, the oldest architectural firm in the East Bay, are the principals (from left) Christopher P. "Kit" Ratcliff, AIA, the third generation of the family in the concern; Syed V. Husain, AIA; Burns Cadwalader, FAIA; and Don T. Kasamoto, AIA.

still maintains a small clientele and serves on the board of directors for The Ratcliff Architects.

The firm's devotion to civic projects and civic improvement is a tradition that is carried on to this day. The firm now focuses on institutional work, such as hospitals, university buildings, and state, county, and municipal structures. Currently the firm is working on

One of the major projects undertaken by The Ratcliff Architects was a thorough renovation of Oakland's Henry J. Kaiser Convention Center. This photo shows the detail in one of the exterior niches featuring allegorical figures.

projects with a total value of $300 million, and was recently named seventh-largest architectural firm in the San Francisco Bay Area, with more than 70 employees. The largest project to date is the $50-million Life Sciences Building renovation at the University of California in Berkeley, which includes a 60,000-square-foot library and 80,000 square feet of new construction. Additional projects include the $33-million Science Facilities Complex for University of Oregon, Eugene; various renovations and additions at Children's Hospital, Oakland; $26-million Foothill Student Housing, the largest housing project undertaken by UC Berkeley in 10 years; and Terminal II for Metropolitan Oakland International Airport, which recently won an Award for Excellence in Design from the East Bay Chapter of the American Institute of Architects. The award-winning firm continues to maintain a diverse project portfolio and is sensitive to surrounding neighborhoods, community, and Alameda County's planning and architectural needs.

"Three basic ideas—diversity, quality, and responsiveness—have helped the firm survive and prosper," notes Kit Ratcliff. "Excellence in design involves taking the time to learn about our clients and understand their goals. A working partnership fosters creative solutions to complex problems. We believe in an aggressively innovative approach to design and project management."

The handsome, $17-million Terminal II building at Oakland's International Airport was designed by The Ratcliff Architects and drew high praise from Allen Temko, the Chronicle's *architectural critic, who described the new commuter terminal as "just about the finest facility of its kind in the country." Photo by Andrew McKinney*

C.P. BANNON MORTUARY

A monument to Charles Patrick Bannon, who began life as a master pattern-maker, is the handsome, block-long C.P. Bannon Mortuary at 6800 East 14th Street, Oakland. The organization marked its 62nd year in business in 1988. The knowledgeable have described the Bannon Mortuary as "one of the largest and most beautiful establishments in California."

A family business, four of Bannon's daughters—the fifth passed away—still operate the firm. Mrs. Dorothy K. Bell is the president; Mrs. Katherine Reboli, who once was a theater organist, presides at either of the two pipe organs; Anna Bannon is the receptionist; and Mrs. Evelyn P. Johnson is office manager and handles any cosmetic work necessary.

A native of Philadelphia, Bannon learned the pattern-maker's trade there and later was transferred to Oakland. He developed a new circle of friends, among whom was a funeral director. During the devastating influenza epidemic that swept the nation in 1918, the mortician asked Bannon to assist him. That brief introduction into the field led Bannon to give serious thought to entering it himself.

In 1926, with virtually no knowledge of the work, Bannon acquired a little candy store building on the site where the mortuary still stands, dismantled the store, and started construction. He made a rough sketch of what he wanted, for Bannon was a shrewd man with good, innovative ideas. The architect took it from there.

The long, rambling two-story building contains three air-conditioned chapels and four reposing rooms. A colonial entrance gives access to the chapels, two of which are of 500-person capacity. The exterior of the building is bathed by floodlights at night.

In the 38 years that Charles Patrick Bannon spent in building up his C.P. Bannon Mortuary in East Oakland, his unfailing assistant was his wife, Anna, who preceded him in death.

The wall of one of the large chapels is of plate glass from floor to ceiling, and those attending a funeral can look out on a tranquil, cloistered garden complete with a placid pool, waterfalls, a miniature forest, and a profusion of flowers. Colored lights illuminate the scene at night.

There have been occasions, Bell recalls, when seven or eight funerals have been held at the mortuary in one day. The funeral for Max Baer, the 1934-1935 heavyweight boxing champion, was held there in 1959, and there have been rites for centenarians as well as in-

Seated at his desk is Charles Patrick Bannon, founder of the well-known C.P. Bannon Mortuary in East Oakland. Bannon began his working career as a pattern-maker. He died in 1964 at the age of 87 and had worked every day to within two weeks of his death.

fants.

"The funeral field has undergone some profound changes in the past 20 years," Bell concludes, "but our business carries on much the same. Families in our area want the traditional, time-honored full-scale funeral with massive quantities of flowers."

AAAAA RENT-A-SPACE

AAAAA Rent-A-Space self storage is, according to the founder, "the largest owner-operated self-storage facility in California" and probably has reached this position by its firm belief in saturation-level advertising. Here a billboard provides a visual incentive for AAAAA Rent-A-Space.

H. James Knuppe, at age 58, has done tolerably well for a fellow who got out of the Army in 1950, fired old steam locomotives on the four-to-midnight shift, and then, in his spare time, built family homes, town houses, condominiums, and apartment houses.

After that, to "keep from losing his touch," the man who piloted his own plane around the world a few years ago and came in second in a 1987 Paris-to-Peking air race, founded the AAAAA Rent-A-Space self-storage firm in 1971. He believes that it is the "largest owner-operated self-storage facility in California."

Michael Knuppe, his son, age 35, is gradually taking over the helm as co-owner and director of management of the company that, in addition to its award-winning headquarters at 2000 Doolittle Drive, San Leandro, has nine Bay Area branches and another under construction on Maui, Hawaii, under the watchful eye of the firm's founder.

The company, whose motto is "store it yourself," and which, in its saturation-level advertising trumpets that it offers a "full-service self-storage place," has statistics to back up its pre-eminence: Including Hawaii, it offers 15,000 retail storage spaces in 70 different sizes encompassing one million square feet. The San Leandro headquarters alone, "one of the world's largest," has 3,069 storage spaces covering 300,000 square feet on eight acres. The firm has some 10,000 customers.

The old concept of the multistoried, monolithic "storage warehouse," where men in white jumpers with the company name embroidered on their backs kept track of inventories and levied a fee each time a customer wanted to "visit" his belongings is "over and passe," Michael Knuppe opines. Self-storage came of age roughly 25 years ago.

"We are, in a sense, a public service-oriented business," Michael Knuppe observes. Customers have their own lock and key for their storage space, and access to the storage area is available from 7 a.m. to 7 p.m., seven days a week, through an electronic code actuating card that triggers an automatic electric gate.

What do customers store? A gallimaufry of items, such as out-of-season sports equipment, memorabilia "you can't bear to part with," and things you bought, don't need, but want to hang on to. Knuppe emphasizes an even more important concept: "the family transition idea—divorce situations, California families moving and on the go, job changes, guests in the home, and, most important, firms that need to store surplus inventory. You might say the company is California's attic."

Asked about any oddball requests for space, Knuppe recalls, that, "Well, there was this fellow with 11 children. He rented a 6-foot by 10-foot space, moved in bookshelves, an easy chair, and a reading lamp. When the bedlam became unbearable, he shifted to his rent-a-space reading room."

U.S. WINDPOWER, INC.

U.S. Windpower, Inc., operates 3,400 wind turbines in Alameda County's blustery Altamont Pass region, generating electricity for the Pacific Gas and Electric Company. The firm is the single-largest producer of wind-generated electricity in the world. The turbines, on their 60-foot tripod towers, are powered by a variable-pitch, three-blade rotor.

U.S. Windpower, Inc., is a leading energy technology company in the independent power supply industry. Founded in 1974, the firm has evolved from a small engineering, research, and development operation into the largest developer and operator of wind-powered electric generating plants in the world. The company has controlled the development of its market through involvement in every aspect of its business. U.S. Windpower designs and manufactures their wind turbines, and constructs, operates, and maintains the wind-powered generating plants.

The concept of a Windplant originated with U.S. Windpower and was based on the idea that an array of several hundred wind turbines, interconnected by a computerized communications network, could be operated as a single power plant. U.S. Windpower has a strong meteorological department and a sophisticated understanding of the wind that "fuels" the Windplant. This allows U.S. Windpower to predict long-term energy output and provide the Windplant owner with a unique energy production warranty.

The firm, with corporate headquarters in San Francisco, produced more than 50 percent of the wind-generated electricity purchased by the Pacific Gas and Electric Company in 1987; more than one-quarter of California's wind-power in the past six years has been generated by U.S. Windpower; and the company has acquired a comprehensive engineering data base through 18 million hours of equipment operation. Cumulatively, the firm has generated more than one billion kilowatt-hours of electricity during the period 1982 to 1987.

People often say, "I never see the windmills in the Altamont Pass turning." The probability of finding windmills turning varies with time of day and season. The climatology in the Altamont Pass provides predictable thermal winds during the summer months of May through September. The winds typically pick up in the early afternoon hours (as the hot air rises in the Central Valley and draws the cool, marine air inland) and will blow throughout the afternoon and evening. If the machines are not turning on a windy summer afternoon, there is either too much wind or they are down for maintenance.

During the winter months, the winds are frequently from the north and run parallel to the strings of windmills that are sited for the prevailing summer winds from the southwest. With northerly winds, operation is limited to one out of every three or four windmills because of the downwind effect on adjacent machines.

U.S. Windpower is one of 20 wind energy companies represented in the Altamont Pass. The turbines look distinctively different and are designed to operate under different wind conditions. The U.S. Windpower turbine produces power in winds ranging from 12 to 44 miles per hour.

The Altamont Pass has served as a model for the wind energy industry worldwide. The technical and operations experience of U.S. Windpower, Inc., has validated the technology and introduced an attractive and economic option for utility power generation.

This photo shows one of U.S. Windpower's "windsmiths" performing routine preventive maintenance atop a 60-foot tripod tower.

DAVID D. BOHANNON ORGANIZATION

Here is a home typical of those built by the David D. Bohannon Organization at San Lorenzo Village during World War II. During construction of the first 1,329 homes on the site, the completion rate was approximately one or more an hour. The village is alive and well with 5,547 homes today.

David D. Bohannon, who estimates he has built perhaps 20,000 homes in his lifetime, ramrodded the building of the novel San Lorenzo Village project during the frenetic days of World War II. Using new methods, he delivered three-bedroom homes at the rate of one or more an hour. In the years after he had left the project, 14 other builders continued the construction using varying techniques.

San Lorenzo Village, the "scientifically planned model community" of 5,547 homes that sprouted up almost overnight on the site of a sleepy hamlet of some 100 people, still stands as "the nation's best privately constructed World War II residential project."

The genius and driving force behind it all was David Dewey Bohannon, or "Big Dave" as many knew him, the president of the David D. Bohannon Organization, which was churning out attractive three-bedroom homes at the rate of one or more an hour in 1944-1945. Ground breaking for the first 1,329-home tract in the novel community occurred on May 18, 1944. The last home was completed on December 15, 1944, setting a record in wartime for private residential construction. The site was the old H.T. Smyth ranch.

It was the apparent answer to the Great American Dream. Just pay $300 down and move right in to a spanking new $5,950 home; or rent it for $50 per month with the option of having the rent payments apply to eventual purchase. In fact, the War Production Board (WPB) was very particular about that—it required that a certain percentage of the homes had to be rented. At San Lorenzo Village, some two-thirds of the homes fell into that category.

"In planning San Lorenzo Village," declares Bohannon, who celebrated his 90th birthday in May 1988, "we did not intend to be satisfied merely to supply shelter. We resolved, in spite of wartime restrictions, to provide quality houses that would become real and enduring homes."

How was it all done? Through something revolutionary called the California Method. Instead of building houses one at a time in the old, traditional custom-made way, Big Dave set up a "cutting yard" on site, where raw lumber (he bought lumber and shingle mills and 20,000 acres of timber) moved along roller tracks to power saws and planers, and was transformed into studs, joists, bridging, and rafters. Then entire walls and other components were assembled, lifted by crane, and hauled to the lot. Ditching machines prepared 25 foundations per day. Sidewalks and curbs were poured at the rate of 1,000 feet per day. Claims Bohannon, "A carpenter working on a house built by the California Method never had to look at a blueprint." The labor force at the village site numbered 2,500.

The master builder—he estimates he has built some 20,000 homes in his lifetime—sold all he constructed at San Lorenzo Village. The village commercial district is his continuing stake; he rents or leases those properties.

San Lorenzo Village, which still resists annexation or incorporation, has come a long way since the days when Jedediah Smith, the fur trapper and explorer, camped nearby in 1827; "squatters" settled in the area in 1851-1852 and called it Squatterville; and, in 1913 or 1914, reportedly, when one of California's last gun duels was fought between two Chinese "in front of Bill Smyth's blacksmith shop."

ROBINSON-COHN AND COMPANY

A mother-son insurance agency that began quite modestly in an East Oakland home 41 years ago is still very much a family business and, in 1986, had property and casualty billings representing $3.5 million in premium volume.

It is Robinson-Cohn and Company, now occupying some 2,800 square feet of space in a large bank building at 14895 East 14th Street, San Leandro. The firm, presided over by Brooklyn-born Ernestine Cohn, widow of Bernard "Barney" Cohn, one of the co-founders, was operated in another location—the Cohn home at 1773-139th Avenue, San Leandro—while the family was growing up. Cohn is now the grandmother of three.

"While Lonnie, our daughter, and the two boys, Laurence and Neil, were growing up, we built an office behind the home," Cohn, a keen, perceptive businesswoman, recalls. "In that way, the kids were always close, and they could call me on the intercom.

"Now Neil, the youngest, is vice-president in charge of marketing and sales and the 'star salesman'; Laurence is a director; Lonnie, although she is not actively associated with the firm, is the corporate secretary; and Laurence's wife, Carol, is a vice-president."

The thriving insurance agency, which was incorporated in 1981, was founded by Barney Cohn and his mother, the late Celia Robinson, in 1946 after Cohn got out of the service. Celia's late husband, Louis Cohn, entered the fire and casualty business in the late 1920s. One of his original clients is still with the agency. From the very start the concern prospered; after five moves to new quarters, the agency located on San Leandro's East 14th Street.

The year 1981 was important for another reason; it was then that the agency acquired the Damiani insurance firm and, in addition, doubled its business volume for the year. Robinson-Cohn writes insurance with more than 100 firms.

Neil Cohn and Ernestine Cohn, principals in Robinson-Cohn and Company.

Cohn, who gives full credit to her late husband for enlarging and diversifying the business, met him at a wedding party in September 1950; they became engaged in November; and the wedding took place in January 1951. She was working for an insurance company at the time and attending the University of California.

Cohn, behind her L-shape desk piled high with insurance papers and reference data and ringed by computers and office machines, is a past president of the Southern Alameda County Chapter of the Professional Insurance Agents and is a member of the Society of Certified Insurance Counselors, the Independent Insurance Agents and Brokers Association, and the Western Association of Insurance Brokers. Other family members are similarly associated.

In 1853, 13 individuals combined to insure the life of William Gybbons of London, and records show the insurance profession dates back at least 600 years. Robinson-Cohn and Company carries on in this time-honored tradition in the twentieth century.

L.M.L. REAL ESTATE DEVELOPMENT COMPANY

Though Jack London Square, Chinatown, and the Rotunda get most of the publicity, the Oakland Renaissance is not confined to the downtown area. Fruitvale and East Oakland, once run-down commercial areas, are also blossoming into bustling business and residential centers, rejuvenated by a new group of developers who believe in the future of these areas.

One such up-and-coming firm, L.M.L. Real Estate Development Company, has been a leader in changing the face of Fruitvale. Through extensive acquisition and renovation programs, the company is creating business and housing opportunities for many Oakland residents.

Founded in 1976 by current president Raymond J. Castor, L.M.L. was

These before and after photographs show the metamorphosis of the L.M.L Real Estate Development Company's Fruitvale Center, from some run-down storefronts (below) with the upper floors vacant, to a modern, unified building group (bottom) stretching over almost a half-block.

named after its first large building acquisition, the Lake Merritt Lodge. Since that time the firm has acquired and renovated more than 50 buildings in East Oakland, the Fruitvale District, and downtown. Today L.M.L. buildings comprise 2 million square feet of rentable space and house 1,000 commercial and residential tenants.

One of L.M.L.'s most important projects is the St. Joseph's Professional Center in Fruitvale. Designated an official landmark, the five-story redbrick structure housed St. Joseph's Home for the Aged for more than six decades before falling into disrepair and closing down. Today, after L.M.L.'s extensive renovation, the center contains 76,000 square feet of modern medical space and is one of the vital business hubs in the district.

Other current Fruitvale development projects include Oakland Hospital, a once vacant bank building at East 14th Street and Fruitvale Avenue, and Fruitvale Center. The center is a row of

four buildings that house 11 retail stores and service businesses with 21 refurbished apartments on the second story.

Since its acquisition of Eastmont, the only regional mall in the Oakland area, L.M.L. has worked diligently to improve the various demographic and economic conditions of East Oakland. The mall provides more than 1,300 jobs, convenient shops, and services to the local community.

In acquiring and developing properties, L.M.L. uses its own construction firm to handle remodeling chores and also manages its own properties. The firm's strong "hands-on" approach emanates from Castor, whose real estate career began in 1972 when he bought his first residential property and renovated it himself. Employed as a restaurant supply manager during the day he worked on the house at night, eventually selling it for a profit and launching his future in real estate development.

Headquartered in downtown Oakland in the Latham Square Building, another L.M.L. renovation project, the company employs a staff of 60, many of whom have been with the firm for years. As owner of Oakland Hospital, which the company is revitalizing into a high-quality community health care facility, L.M.L. is also responsible for the livelihoods of 300 medical and administrative staff.

In addition to the obvious real estate benefits that L.M.L. affords the city of Oakland, the company believes in active community support and participation. Many nonprofit and charitable organizations, such as Bay Area Community Services and Catholic Charities, pay reduced rents in L.M.L. buildings. L.M.L. is also an active participant in several civic programs and community projects.

With a strong belief in Oakland's business future, L.M.L. Real Estate Development Company will continue to leave its mark on the city for years to come.

THRIFTY CAR RENTAL

With its half-century-old origins in the family-owned downtown Oakland automobile parking business, the franchised Thrifty Car Rental company, with two outlets in the city, is showing steady annual growth.

The firm's co-owners and managers are David M. Flett and Leland Douglas. Rent-a-Car branches are situated at 111-98th Avenue and 1432 Harrison Street, Oakland. They operate under the flag of the worldwide Thrifty Rent-a-Car System, Inc., with headquarters in Tulsa, Oklahoma.

Situated within 1.5 miles of Oakland International Airport, the 98th Avenue outlet caters to air travelers. It furnishes ample parking facilities for those who prefer the more moderate rates over those charged at the airport

parking lot and, in addition, provides a unique 24-hour-a-day shuttle bus service to and from the airport. This amenity is in addition, of course, to a full-service auto rental business featuring a complete line of cars from subcompacts to luxury models.

Because the firm is part of a nationwide organization, it is possible for customers who wish to drive one-way to say, Los Angeles, San Diego, or Sacramento, to be accommodated. Thrifty outlets in those cities simply route the cars back to Oakland. Flett adds that his firm also makes credit cards avail-

Thrifty Car Rental offers a complete line of cars from subcompacts to luxury models. In addition, Thrifty provides a unique 24-hour-a-day shuttle bus service to and from the airport.

able to valued customers and that out-of-town reservations can be made through the company's 800 number.

"This is a very competitive and service-oriented business," Flett observes, "where we try hard to build customer loyalty. We stress courtesy among our 20 employees and a willingness to accept criticism without argument. The new Thrifty image is taking hold and firmly positioning us to compete. More and more people are beginning to understand that you can supplement a household or college car with a rental car from one of our outlets."

The roots of this family business lie in the Douglas Parking Company, which Flett's uncle, Sanford Douglas, established a half-century ago.

SHATTUCK HOTEL

Berkeley's landmark Shattuck Hotel was built in two successive units. This, the first, was situated at the south corner of Shattuck Avenue and Allston Way. It formally opened December 15, 1910. An annex, extending the hotel to Shattuck and Kittredge, was completed in 1914.

When Berkeley's Shattuck Hotel, the city's major downtown hostelry, formally opened on December 15, 1910, Noah W. Gray, then the manager, declared: "'Meet me at the Shattuck' is an expression that I hope all our people will get in the habit of using."

Gray's hopes were fulfilled for, increasingly over the intervening 77 years, travelers from all parts of the world as well as those living nearby have patronized the hotel, which now has official landmark status.

In the long tally of distinguished guests who registered at the hotel have been Cornelius Vanderbilt, Jr., film stars Dana Andrews and Robert Young, and the entire casts of "Teahouse of the August Moon," "South Pacific," "Oklahoma," and "Country Girl." It has been the state headquarters for the California Federation of Women's Clubs, and many of the city's service clubs meet there regularly. Crusty Joaquin Miller, the bearded Poet of the Sierra, was one of the opening-night speakers.

The full-service hotel, with its appurtenant storefront revenue-producing properties, occupies an entire downtown Berkeley block. The five-story Spanish Renaissance-style building, one of the first reinforced concrete structures erected in the city, is bounded by Shattuck Avenue, Allston and Harold ways, and Kittredge Street. It has 175 rooms. The J.F. Hink and Son department store was a major lessee for some 60 years.

The hotel underwent a $2-million 1987 renovation, one of several it has passed through in a continuing modernization process. A licensed architect, owner Eli Cukierman, was well qualified to undertake overall supervision of the job. In keeping with the times, when the hotel was built it boasted mahogany and Circassian walnut interior finish and birdseye maple flooring in the dining and ballrooms. The 1910 lobby was eye-catching with its black marble pillars, set off by cream-color walls. In the 1930s, and again in a 1980s revival, tea dances were held in the 3,000-square-foot ballroom.

Testifying to the hotel's insistence on color-theme rooms, a copy of a 1910 issue of the *Western Hotel Reporter* reported that if, for instance, a given room had a blue color scheme, "you will find that the rim around the water pitcher, cuspidor, and match stand are also blue."

The hotel was built on the northern portion of the extensive homesite of the late Francis K. Shattuck, a pioneer Berkeleyan who was active in politics, business, and banking. The hotel was named in his honor by William H. Woolsey, president of the Hotel Shat-

Two views of the Shattuck Hotel today.

tuck Association formed in 1907 to undertake construction. Woolsey's associates included Addison W. Naylor, pioneer banker; William H. Waste, who later became chief justice of the California Supreme Court; and B.F. Brooks.

Not long after the first unit of the big hotel was completed in 1910, it became evident that more space was needed. Consequently, an annex extending south to Kittredge Street was undertaken. It was completed in 1914.

This led to a competition of superlatives, with one newspaper reporting the hotel was "the longest building in any city about the bay . . . being five feet longer than the Emporium on Market Street, San Francisco." Not to be outdone, another paper declared it was "the longest building in the state . . . and one of the most imposing on the east side of the bay."

During the period from December 7-16, 1910, there was a different event dealing with the hotel opening each day. On December 7, for instance, the first guests registered—a Mrs. Foster of Berkeley and her friend, Mrs. J.B. Hume, former president of the Bay Fed-

eration of Women's Clubs. The big chamber of commerce banquet was held December 15. John A. Britton, president of the Pacific Gas and Electric Company, recalled he had known Shattuck well and declared:

"No better tribute could have been paid to the man through the naming of that broad, beautiful thoroughfare (Shattuck Avenue) for him. It typifies the man as do the straight and powerful columns of this stately building in which we now sit and which also bears his name."

The hotel and its commercial properties have undergone at least eight changes in lessees or owners over the years. Probably the shift surrounded by the most titillating gossip was that in which William W. Whitecotton assumed control. A big sign, "The Hotel Whitecotton," went up immediately despite the hotel's long and favored association with the Shattuck name. Whitecotton came to the hotel as chief clerk about 1919. A romance report-

edly soon developed between him and a wealthy widow. Almost immediately after the wedding the Shattuck Hotel name was retired.

Eli Cukierman became the hotel's sole owner in 1980.

THUNDERBIRD PROPERTIES, INC.

Oakland's modern Boatel-a Waterfront Inn on the famed Jack London Waterfront claims a close link with the city's storied past and the days of gold. Its three-story building at 88 Jack London Square is situated precisely in the area where some 75 "squatters" on a Spanish land grant established the hamlet of Contra Costa in 1850-1851. Later it became Oakland.

Turning to the here and now, Clyde R. Gibb's Boatel-a Waterfront Inn, a unit in the growing Thunderbird Inns and Hotels organization, looks to the future and the completion of the $100-million modernization of the Jack London Waterfront. The Boatel will play a major role in the program: The plans are to double its size, adding 75 rooms along the Oakland Estuary.

The facility is designed so that one may appreciate, in any Boatel room, the tang of salt sea air drifting in the window and the muffled, rhythmic sound of the pulse of a ship's engines somewhere off in the night. That's just a bit of the atmosphere to enjoy at the Boatel. In the daytime, Boatel guests are fascinated by the ever-changing estuary scene with its oceangoing ships, tugs, and pleasure craft, both motorized and sail. There are other benefits—a sunning deck, complete with swimming pool. Nautically themed, the Boatel also boasts four boat slips.

The Boatel's ground breaking was novel. Since some of the structure extends out into the estuary, a piling was spray painted gold and civic dignitaries autographed it before the pile driver moved in.

Guests at the Boatel are close to downtown Oakland and the Convention Center by car or public transportation and shuttle buses go to the Oakland International Airport or Bay Area Rapid Transit (BART) trains that whisk away to San Francisco or the Oakland Coliseum. The Coliseum, in season, is the home of the Oakland Athletics baseball team of the American League and the Golden State Warriors of the National Basketball Association. At nearby Albany is Golden Gate Fields, which offers thoroughbred racing during the state-allotted days. Close by in the Jack London Waterfront area are a variety of fine restaurants.

Thunderbird Inns and Hotels, headquartered at the Jack London Waterfront, is a group of properties consisting of 14 inns and hotels offering pleasant, affordable hospitality to the business traveler and vacationer alike. The properties vary in size and services. There are seven located in the San Francisco Bay Area with four more in Northern California, and one each in Utah, Montana, and Washington.

Gibb's goal for the Thunderbird Inns and Hotels organization is 25 hostelries. In the immediate area, in addition to the Boatel, are the Thunderbird Motor Inn, 233 Broadway, Oakland; the Park Plaza Hotel at the Oakland International Airport; the Hotel Durant in Berkeley; the Thunderbird Motor Inn in Fremont; and two units managed by president Gibb's organization, the Wharf Inn in San Francisco and the Walnut Creek Inn.

Clyde R. Gibb, active in many Oakland civic ventures, is president of the growing Thunderbird Inns and Hotels organization, which numbers among its properties Oakland's modern Boatel Motor Lodge on the famed Jack London Waterfront.

An artist's rendering of the Boatel-a Waterfront Inn. From the sun and swimming pool deck and many of the rooms, guests can enjoy a scenic waterfront view ranging from oceangoing vessels to small sailboats.

OAKLAND CHAMBER OF COMMERCE

William S. Downing is immediate past president and chief executive officer of the 83-year-old Oakland Chamber of Commerce. He sees Oakland as the logical future center of the Bay Area. San Francisco, he says, "has reached the limits of its growth."

Hardly four months old, the Oakland Chamber of Commerce stepped into the gap to supervise and provide relief of all kinds for an estimated 100,000 to 150,000 refugees from the great San Francisco earthquake and fire of April 18, 1906.

Edson F. Adams, a banker who had been installed as chamber president on December 11 of the previous year, supervised the arranging of food and shelter for the displaced transbay residents and even arranged a unique mailing address service in cooperation with the post office for some 3,000 displaced San Francisco businessmen. And although the aid provided was intended to be purely philanthropic, the scriptural precept about casting bread upon the waters was fulfilled as some 65,000 of the refugees remained to become residents of Oakland.

Now 83 years old, the Oakland Chamber of Commerce, with 1,250 members, has broadened its vision beyond the traditional tasks of assisting business and promoting trade. "Our mission is broader now," William S. Downing, immediate past president, observes. "We are involved in other ar-

Edson F. Adams, pioneer Oakland banker, was installed as the first president of the Oakland Chamber of Commerce on December 11, 1905. Four months later the chamber was supervising relief efforts for 100,000 to 150,000 refugees from the San Francisco earthquake and fire.

eas—the schools, arts, and other cultural fields. We are the sole, unified voice for the entire city, not just industry or big business. We speak for neighborhood organizations and individuals also.

"The goal for Oakland and the Oakland Chamber of Commerce is identical: fulfill the city's potential as the commerce and transportation hub of the Bay Area. Four freeways converge here; we are the hub of the Bay Area Rapid Transit District (BART) lines; two transcontinental railroads terminate here; we are one of the largest marine container cargo ports in the nation.

The chamber's predecessors were the Merchants Protective Union, founded in 1870; the Merchants Exchange, 1877-1880; and the Board of Trade, formed in 1886.

The Oakland Chamber of Commerce organizational meeting was held November 11, 1905; incorporation took place November 22, 1905; and the first regular meeting and the installation of officers occurred December 11, 1905. The first assembly rooms were in the old Athenian Club. Now the chamber, with 14 employees, is located at 475-14th Street, an area known as City Center.

In recent years, Downing points out, the chamber has been involved in large-scale civic improvement projects. It spearheaded the drive for the $30-million Coliseum complex, completed in 1966. In the past year it helped produce a favorable vote on Proposition B that provides for a 15-year countywide half-cent sales tax to rehabilitate the Nimitz freeway and aid mass transit.

Says Downing, "We all see great things ahead for Oakland!"

CITY OF OAKLAND—OFFICE OF ECONOMIC DEVELOPMENT AND EMPLOYMENT

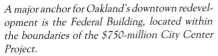

A major anchor for Oakland's downtown redevelopment is the Federal Building, located within the boundaries of the $750-million City Center Project.

Interested in every aspect of Oakland's massive $2-billion urban revitalization program is Mayor Lionel Wilson, who since 1978 has spearheaded the city's economic development commitment and investment.

Moving aggressively on its rapidly rising reputation as the renaissance city of the West, Oakland has embarked upon an unprecedented urban revitalization program that is luring national retailers to the downtown area—building the tax base, increasing business opportunities, and creating jobs. Some say the effort is unmatched by any other city in the nation.

The scope of redevelopment in the city's central sector alone encompasses roughly 930 acres with sweeping East Oakland vistas awaiting similar treatment. It is as though a giant hand has swept away an accumulation of aging, obsolete buildings in a shabby business district and, like magic, replaced them overnight with a bold new Oakland skyline of historically preserved as well as modern architectural wonders.

"Oakland means business. If you haven't seen Oakland lately, you haven't seen Oakland," is the way progressive Mayor Lionel Wilson puts it. Symbolic of the city's commitment to redevelopment was Wilson's cre-

ation of the Office of Economic Development and Employment as a separate department in 1979. During his three-year term, redevelopment has flourished.

Sparkplug for this prodigious facelift is George H. Williams, director of Oakland's Office of Economic Development, who supervises a staff of 90 and scores of projects, and is ever on the lookout for major building tenants. Williams, an architect, explains: "There is an economic shift taking place in the Bay Area, and sitting in the middle of it all is Oakland . . . we're the hub."

To get a handle on the vast proportions of this multi-phased program, whose target extends from the waters of the estuary on the south to about 22 blocks northward, one statistic is worth noting: Oakland's downtown office space has increased from 6.5 million square feet in 1979 to 10 million square feet today.

Oakland, described as "the nation's most integrated city," aims at realizing its fair share of Bay Area growth. Experts say it is one of the West Coast's most underserved and undersold retail markets in the nation.

To quote Mayor Wilson again:

"Oakland is the center of commerce, the Gateway to the Bay Region, and it has the state's best airport. Six major highways, all three transcontinental railroads, and some 1,000 trucking firms or their subsidiaries converge here. It is the main sea terminal for cargo between the western United States and the Pacific Basin, Latin America, and Europe. Oakland is the destination of more than 90 percent of all container cargo coming through the Golden Gate."

While priorities and statistics inevitably change as the redevelopment program goes forward, here are just a few examples of some of the major projects in this $2-billion construction mosaic in which the city and private industry are partners:

Linchpin of the broad-based program is the $750-million, 12-block Oakland City Center Project in the heart of the downtown area. It is a 5-million-square-foot mixed-use complex designed to serve Oakland's growing fi-

nancial community. Focal points will include four plaza areas and a mix of office towers, restaurants, and shops, all linked by a network of interconnecting walkways. City Square—4.5 jewel-like acres within the core of the City Center Project—makes visitors almost forget they are in the center of a big city. There are fountains, waterfalls, inviting benches, tree-lined walks, and a 70-foot glass "beacon" as a special eyecatcher. This part of the project includes 60,000 square feet of shops and 130,000 square feet of offices.

Also located within the City Center boundaries is the $150-million Federal Building. According to OEDE director Williams, "a major milestone for Oakland was our winning bid in the competition with San Francisco for the one-million-square-foot Federal Building. This building could not have

George H. Williams, director of Oakland's Office of Economic Development and Employment, is the key strategist for the city's ambitious $2-billion urban revitalization program.

happened prior to the new surge in development activity."

Approximately 4,500 employees will be housed in the twin 18-story towers (linked by a glazed bridge), a 75-foot-high glazed rotunda, and two 18-story wings to contain a federal courthouse and auditorium-conference center.

As a foil to all this modern architectural glitz is Old Oakland, a 5.7-acre enclave "containing the best examples of Victorian architecture in the western United States" and spanning the period from 1866 to 1933. The clout of the collection is the venerable Henry House, a three-story Italianate built by

Ashmun Henry during the gold and silver excitements. In the same category, at the 122-year-old Arlington, where the old and very new meet, KRON TV-4 has its East Bay bureau with a microwave "dish" on the roof. The buildings are listed on the U.S. Interior Department's Historical Register and will provide some 219,000 square feet of retail and office space.

Bulking large on the revenue-producing horizon is the $300-million regional Retail Center, which contemplates three to five new department stores, as many as 100 shops, and a mix of office buildings, residential development, and parking garages, featuring a 350,000-square-foot multi-level mall.

Also in the spotlight is the Rotunda—an ingeniously devised $55-million reanimation of the old 1912 Kahn's Department Store building with its 5,000-square-foot elliptical dome. This beaux arts structure is being reconfigured to provide a restaurant plaza, three floors of retail shops, and five floors devoted to offices.

Of significance is the $180-million Chinatown project, scheduled for completion in 1991. Containing retail stores, restaurants, a cultural center, a library, and housing, it reflects the Asian cultural influence in the city.

Odds on, Oakland's reclaimed position as the Bay Area's Center of Commerce is here to stay!

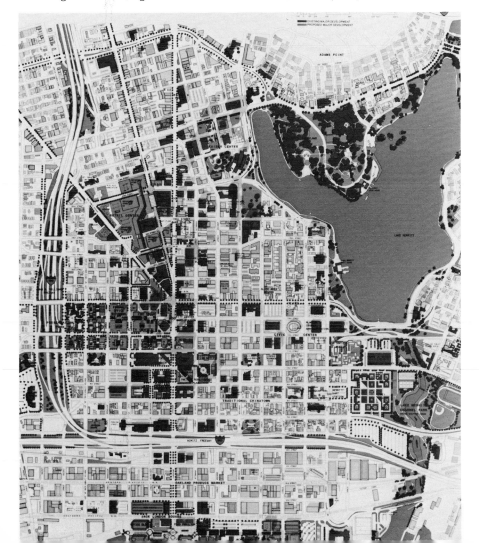

Oakland's central business district is the main focus of the city's $2-billion urban revitalization program.

CONCANNON VINEYARD

Livermore's historic Concannon Vineyard, founded 105 years ago and rich in honors, is undergoing a renaissance of the first order with a distinguished Renaissance Man at the helm.

"I am using," declares Dr. Sergio Traverso, the winery president, winemaker, and co-owner, "traditional French winemaking practices to enable Concannon to produce wine ranking among the best in the world . . . The austere soil and temperate climate in the Livermore Valley provide ideal conditions for the noble grapes used in Concannon's two estate bottled varietal wines—Sauvignon Blanc and Cabernet Sauvignon.

"The complex and elegant wines of Concannon rank among the greatest varietals produced in California. It is the gravelly, pebbled soil in the vineyard that allows Concannon to produce wines of notable character." Chateau-type French oak barrels are used exclusively in the cellar.

At 47 Chilean-born Traverso has a Ph.D. in microbiology from the University of California at Davis, where he once taught in the Department of Enology and Viticulture. At one time he was director of winemaking at Casa Madero in Mexico. Later he was, successively, winemaker at Napa County's Domaine Chandon and Sterling wineries.

At the mention of Napa County, Traverso, a man with an engaging personality, adds an observation: "Our soil is the best in California for growing grapes, better than Napa County's. Our 220-acre vineyard—172 of them planted—is a jewel."

The winery was founded in 1883 by James Concannon. It survived the hardscrabble years of Prohibition by bottling sacramental wines. Seven years ago the Concannon family sold out. The present owners of the winery are Traverso and Deinhard & Co., an old and prestigious family of wine producers in the Rhine and Mosel regions. Affixed to one of the buildings is a

Dr. Sergio Traverso, president, winemaker, and co-owner at the 105-year-old Concannon Vineyard in Livermore, stresses traditional French wine-making practices. He was formerly on the faculty at the University of California at Davis where he taught in the Department of Enology and Viticulture.

bronze plaque marking the antiquity of the winery, placed there by the California State Park Commission in conjunction with Las Positas Parlor No. 96, Native Sons of the Golden West. In the attractive tasting room is a California Historical Society Centennial Business Award and letters from President Ronald Reagan and then-Governor Jerry Brown marking the 100th anniversary of the winery.

Under Traverso's direction, Concannon Vineyard's focus and line of wines has been narrowed. At one time the winery produced more than 18 different wines, but today it makes only five. Traverso is concentrating his talent and energy primarily on the premium varietals of Sauvignon Blanc, Chardonnay, and Cabernet Sauvignon. In fact, he is one of only a few California vintners producing Cabernet Sauvignon exclusively by the Bordelaise method.

Following the strict cellar practices of the Bordelaise technique, Concannon Vineyard's Cabernet is racked barrel to barrel via a hand pump. Most wineries use massive electrical pumps to transfer their wines quickly in the cellars, but Traverso believes that hand pumping his Cabernet has benefits. With a hand pump, the wine is ever so slightly exposed to air, which allows the wine to develop a subtle aroma and soften the wine's natural tannins. Done properly, a Bordelaise-produced Cabernet develops early on into a wine of finesse with rich, velvety texture.

Concannon Vineyard is open daily for tours. Visitors can be assured of a warm welcome at the winery, where you can visit the cellars, taste the wines, and see the gravelly, pebbled soil that produces some of California's finest wines.

In an earlier time, when the tractor was gradually displacing the horse and mule, this view of a young vineyard at Livermore's Concannon Vineyard emphasizes the gravelly, craggy nature of the soil in which the grape vines thrive.

PATRONS

The following individuals, companies, and organizations have made a valuable commitment to the quality of this publication. Windsor Publications and the Alameda County Historical Society gratefully acknowledge their participation in *Alameda County: California Crossroads: An Illustrated History.*

AAAAA Rent-A-Space*
C.P. Bannon Mortuary*
David D. Bohannon Organization*
Boyle, Cowan & Co., Certified Public
        Accountants*
Buttner Pioneer Family-Sunol/1850
City of Oakland-Office of Economic
        Development and Employment*
Civicbank of Commerce
Concannon Vineyard*
Deloitte Haskins & Sells*
Eden Hospital Medical Center*
First American Title Guarantee Co.
Golden Gate Litho
The Hewlett Packard Co.
Holmes Book Co.
Intel Corporation*
L.M.L. Real Estate Development
        Company*
Melrose Lumber & Supply Co.
Mercury Mortgage Service Corp.
Morehouse Foods, Inc.*
Mother's Cake & Cookie Co.*
Mr. & Mrs. Milton Maxwell Newmark
D.W. Nicholson Corporation
Oakland Business Development Corp.
Oakland Chamber of Commerce*
Pasco Scientific
The Ratcliff Architects*
Robinson-Cohn and Company*
Sandia National Laboratories
Sea-Land Service, Inc.
Shattuck Hotel*
Clifton A. Sherwood
Swadley Enterprises*
Thrifty Car Rental*
Thunderbird Properties, Inc.*
The Tribune*
U.S. Windpower, Inc.*
Washington Hospital Healthcare System*

*Partners in Progress of *Alameda County: California Crossroads: An Illustrated History.* The histories of these companies and organizations appear in Chapter 8, beginning on page 99.

The Ladies Aid Society of San Leandro's First Presbyterian Church was photographed in 1895. The society organized bazaars and sewing bees to help the needy and led the local fight against the evils of "demon rum". Courtesy, San Leandro Community Library Center

BIBLIOGRAPHY

Adams, Edson F. *Oakland's Early History*. Oakland: Tribune Publishing Company, 1932.

Alameda-Contra Costa Transit District. "A Pictorial History of Public Transportation in the East Bay." *Transit Times* VI, no. 5, September 1963.

Alameda County Agricultural Fair Association. *1912-1987: Diamond Jubilee Celebration*. Exhibit catalogue.

Alameda County Parks, Recreation, and Historical Commission. *Alameda County Parks, Recreation, and Historic Sites Directory*. Hayward, 1981.

Bagwell, Beth. *Oakland: The Story of a City*. Novato: Presidio Press, 1982.

Baker, Joseph E. *Past and Present of Alameda County*. 2 vols. Chicago: S.J. Clarke Publishing Company, 1914.

Bancroft, Hubert Howe. *History of California*. 7 vols. San Francisco: A.L. Bancroft & Company, 1884-1890.

Bean, Walton and James J. Rawls. *California: An Interpretive History*. 4th ed. New York: McGraw-Hill Book Company, 1983.

Bernhardi, Robert. *The Buildings of Berkeley*. Berkeley: Lederer, Street, and Zeus, 1971.

_____. *The Buildings of Oakland*. Oakland: Forest Hill Press, 1979.

Bohn, Dave. *East of These Golden Shores*. Oakland: Scrimshaw Press, 1971.

Bolton, Herbert Eugene, ed. *Fray Juan Crespi: Missionary Explorer on the Pacific Coast, 1769-1774*. Berkeley: University of California Press, 1927.

Burgess, Sherwood D. "The Forgotten Redwoods of the East Bay." *California Historical Quarterly* 30, no. 1.

California State Department of Natural Resources. *Geologic Guidebook of the San Francisco Bay Counties*. Ed. Olaf P. Jenkins. San Francisco, 1952.

Camp, Charles L. *Earth Song: A Prologue to History*. Palo Alto: American West, 1952.

Cardwell, Kenneth H. *Bernard Maybeck: Artisan, Architect, Artist*. Santa Barbara and Salt Lake City: Peregrine Smith, 1977.

Collins, Michael. "Our Planet: Fragile Gem in the Universe." *Birmingham Post Herald*, March 1, 1972.

Conmy, Peter T. *The Athenian-Nile Club: 100 Years of Genial Hours*. Ed. Llewellyn E. Thompson II. Oakland, 1983.

_____. *The Beginnings of Oakland*. Oakland: Oakland Public Library, 1961.

Connor, Ann W., ed. *Saga of San Leandro*. Cupertino: California History Center, 1973.

Covell, Paul F. *People Are for the Birds: The Adventures and Observations of the West's First Municipal Park Naturalist at America's First Waterfowl Refuge—Lake Merritt, Oakland*. Oakland: Western Interpretive Press, 1978.

Cowan, Robert Granis. *Ranchos of California*. Fresno: Academic Library Guild, 1956.

Crocker, Florence B. *Who Made Oakland*. Oakland: Clyde Dalton, 1925.

Daniels, Roger and Spencer C. Olin, Jr. *Racism in California: A Reader in the History of Oppression*. New York: Macmillan Company, 1972.

Davis, William Heath. *Seventy-Five Years in California*. Ed. Harold A. Small. 3rd ed. San Francisco: John Howell Books, 1967.

DeMoro, Harre. "Amid Nostalgia for the Old Ferries and Trains." *San Francisco Business Journal*, February 23, 1981.

_____. "The Big Red Cars." *The Western Railroader* 19, no. 7, May 1956.

_____. "The Conversion of the Key System." *National Railway Bulletin* 44, no. 6, 1979.

Dillon, Richard. *High Steel: Building the Bridges Across San Francisco Bay*. Millbrae: Celestial Arts, 1979.

Early Days in the Livermore-Amador Valley. Hayward: Alameda County School Department, 1973.

Eden Writers. *Hayward: The First 100 Years*. Oakland: Color Art Press, 1975.

Everett, Amelia D. "The Ship 'Brooklyn'." *California Historical Society Quarterly* XXXVII (September 1958): 229-240.

Fay, James S., Anne G. Lipow, and Stephanie W. Fay. *California Almanac, 1986-87*. Novato: Presidio Press

and Pacific Data Resources, 1985.

Fibell, Pearl Randolph. *The Peraltas: Spanish Pioneers and First Family of the East Bay*. Oakland: Peralta Hospital, 1971.

Field, Connie, director and producer. *The Life and Times of Rosie the Riveter*. Emeryville: Clarity Educational Film Productions, 1972. Film.

Flint, Leslie. *The Heart of Oakland: A Walking Guide to Lake Merritt*. Oakland: Camron-Stanford House Preservation Association, 1978.

Franks, Robert. "Berkeley." Unpublished manuscript. Watsonville, 1988.

Freeman, Leslie J. *Alameda County Past and Present*. San Leandro, 1946.

Freudenheim, Leslie Mandelson and Elisabeth Sacks Sussman. *Building with Nature: Roots of the San Francisco Bay Region Tradition*. Santa Barbara and Salt Lake City: Peregrine Press, 1973.

Gebhard, David, et al. *A Guide to Architecture in San Francisco and Northern California*. 2nd ed. Santa Barbara and Salt Lake City: Peregrine Press, 1982.

Gibson, Otis. *The Chinese in America*. Cincinnati: Hitchcock and Walker, 1877.

Glanz, Rudolph. *The Jews of California from the Discovery of Gold until 1880*. New York: Southern California Jewish Historical Society, 1960.

Gonsalves, L., and Winfield Scott, eds. "Portuguese Colonies in California." *Out West* (April 1911):290-293.

Gordon, Tim. "Geology of the East Bay." *Regional Parks Log*. Oakland: East Bay Regional Park District, 1987.

Halley, William. *The Centennial Yearbook of Alameda County, California*. Oakland: William Halley, 1876.

Hamilton, Mildred. "A Woman Above All Others." *San Francisco Examiner* Centennial Edition, March 1, 1987.

Hart, James D. *A Companion to California*. Berkeley: University of California Press, 1987.

Hausler, Donald. "Blacks in Early Oakland." Unpublished monograph, 1980. Oakland Public Library, Oakland History Room.

Heisler, Robert F. *The Costanoan Indians*. Cupertino: California History

Center, 1974.

Hinkel, Edgar J. and William C. McCann. *History of Rural Alameda County.* Oakland: Works Progress Administration, 1937.

_____. *Oakland, 1852-1938: Some Phases of the Social, Political, and Economic History of Oakland, California.* 2 vols. Oakland: Works Progress Administration, 1939.

Hoover, Mildred Brooks, Hero Eugene Rensch, and Edith Grace Rensch. *Historic Spots in California.* 3rd ed., rev. by William N. Abeloe. Stanford: Stanford University Press, 1966.

Hutchison, W.H. *California: The Golden Shore by the Sundown Sea.* Belmont: Star Publishing Company, 1984.

Kinnard, Lawrence. *History of the S.F. Bay Region.* 3 vols. New York: Lewis Historical Publishing Company, 1966.

Kitchell, Mark. *Berkeley in the Sixties* (working title). January 1988. Film.

Lafler, Henry Anderson. *Alameda County.* Oakland: Alameda County Board of Supervisors, 1915.

Lai, Him Mark, Joe Huang, and Don Wong. *The Chinese of America, 1785-1980.* San Francisco: Chinese Culture Foundation, 1980.

"Landmarks and Preservation Districts." Typescript. Oakland: Landmarks Preservation Advisory Board, 1984.

Longstreth, Richard W. *Julia Morgan, Architect.* Berkeley: Berkeley Architectural Heritage Association, 1977.

McArdle, Phil. *Exactly Opposite the Golden Gate.* Berkeley: Berkeley Historical Society, 1983.

MacGregor, Bruce. *The Centennial History of Newark.* Newark: Newark Days Bicentennial Committee, 1976.

Ma, Eve Armentrout and Jeong Huei Ma. *Chinese of Oakland: Unsung Builders.* Oakland: Chinese Historical Research Committee, n.d.

Margolin, Malcolm. *The Ohlone Way: Indian Life in the San Francisco-Monterey Bay Area.* Berkeley: Heyday Books, 1978.

Mathes, W. Michael. *Missions.* San Francisco: California Historical Society, 1980.

Merlin, Imelda. *Alameda: A Geographical History.* Alameda: Friends of the Alameda Free Library, 1977.

Merritt, Frank Clinton. *History of Alameda County, California.* 2 vols. Chicago: A.J. Clarke Publishing Company, 1928.

Mitchell, Margaretta K. "Dance for Life: Isadora Duncan and the Temple of Wings." Berkeley: Elysian Editions, 1985.

Monteagle, F.J. *Coney Island of the West.* Oakland: East Bay Regional Park District, 1977.

_____. *Lively Century: San Leandro Bay.* Oakland: East Bay Regional Park District, 1978.

Mott, Frank K. *A Review of Municipal Activities in the City of Oakland, California, 1905-1915.* Oakland: City of Oakland, 1915.

Oakeshott, Gordon B. *California's Changing Landscapes: A Guide to the Geology of the State.* New York: McGraw Hill, 1971.

Oakland Board of Port Commissioners. *Port of Oakland: 60 Years; A Chronicle of Progress, 1987.*

Oakland Chamber of Commerce. *Alameda County: The Bright Side of the Bay.* Oakland: Registry Publishing, 1985.

_____. *Greater Oakland, 1911.* Oakland, 1911.

Oakland Daily Evening Tribune. Special Illustrated Editions, 1887, 1888, 1890.

Oakland Tribune. "Alameda County: The Eden of the Pacific, the Flower Garden of California." 1898.

_____. "Centennial Edition: Oakland, 1852-1952." May 1, 1952.

_____. "The Knave." Columns by Leonard Verbarg on Oakland history, 1952-1972.

_____. Yearbooks. 1911 to 1949.

Pattiani, Evelyn Craig. *Queen of the Hills: The Story of Piedmont.* Fresno: Academy Library Guild, 1953.

Pettit, George A. *Berkeley: The Town and Gown of It.* Berkeley: Howell-North Books, 1973.

Pitt, Leonard. *California Controversies: Major Issues in the History of the State.* San Rafael: ETRI Publishing Company, 1985.

_____. *The Decline of the Californios: A Social History of the Spanish-Speaking Californians, 1846-1890.* Berkeley and Los Angeles: University of California Press, 1970.

Pleasanton Times. Special Edition. August 13, 1910.

Pressler, Jerome D. "Landscape Modification through Time: The Coyote Hills; Alameda County, California." M.A. thesis, California State University Hayward, 1973.

Putnam, Jackson K. *Modern California Politics, 1917-1980.* San Francisco: Boyd & Fraser Publishing Company, 1980.

Rand McNally Guide to San Francisco, Oakland, Berkeley, and the Environs of the Bay Cities. San Francisco: Rand McNally and Company, 1927.

Rather, Lois. *Oakland's Image: A History of Oakland, California.* Oakland: Rather Press, 1972.

Rawls, James U. *Indians of California: The Changing Image.* Norman: University of Oakland Press, 1984.

Rosenbaum, Fred. *Free to Choose: The Making of a Jewish Community in the American West.* Berkeley: Judah L. Magnes Memorial Museum, 1976.

Sandoval, John S. *The History of Washington Township.* Hayward: Mt. Eden Publishers, 1985.

Scott, Mel. *The San Francisco Bay Area: A Metropolis in Perspective.* 2nd ed. Berkeley: University of California Press, 1985.

Shaffer, Harry. *A Garden Grows in Eden: The Centennial Story of San Leandro.* San Leandro: San Leandro Historical-Centennial Committee, 1972.

Shinn, Charles H. "The Alvarado Squatters' League." *Out West* XXVI, January 1907.

Soito, Patricia. *A Hundred Years of Pleasanton: The Most Desperate Town in the West.* San Francisco: F. Phillips & Van Orden Company, 1949.

Stadtman, Verne A., ed. *The Centennial Record of the University of California.* Berkeley: University of California, 1967.

Stein, Mimi. *A Vision Achieved: Fifty Years of the East Bay Regional Park District.* Oakland: East Bay Regional

Park District, 1984.

Stirton, R.A. "Cenozoic Animal Remains from the San Francisco Bay Region." *Bulletin of the Department of Geological Sciences* no. 13. Berkeley: University of California Press, 1937.

Stuart, Reginald Ray. *Corridor Country: An Interpretive History of the Amador-Livermore Valley.* Livermore: Amador-Livermore Valley Historical Society, 1966.

Taylor, William. *California Life.* New York: Carlton and Porter, 1858.

Thompson, Thomas Hinckley and Albert Augustus West. *Historical Atlas of Alameda County, California.* 1878. Reprint. Fresno: Valley Publishers, 1976.

Trimble, Paul C. *Interurban Railways of the Bay Area.* Fresno: Valley Publishers, 1977.

Tsuji, Kenyu T., ed. *Buddhist Churches of America: 75 Years' History.* Chicago: Norbar, Inc., 1974.

Verbarg, Leonard. *Celebrities at Your Doorstep.* Oakland: Alameda County Historical Society, 1972.

Vigness, Paul G. *History of Alameda.* Alameda: Arthur H. Cawston, 1939.

Ward, Charles. "Reminiscences." *Society of California Pioneers Publications.* San Francisco, 1949.

Weber, David. *Oakland: Hub of the West.* Tulsa: Continental Heritage Press, 1981.

Wood, M.W. *History of Alameda County.* 1883. Reprint. Oakland: Holmes Book Company, 1969.

Writers' Program of the Works Progress Administration. *Berkeley: The First Seventy-Five Years.* Berkeley: Gillick Press, 1941.

_____. *San Francisco: The Bay and Its Cities.* New York: Hastings House, 1940.

Zobell, Albert L. "The Mormon Church in Early California." *The Improvement Era.* Oakland Temple Issue, 1964.

INDEX